How To Prune
Fruit Trees
AND Roses

UPDATED EDITION

How To Prune Fruit Trees *by R. Sanford Martin updated, revised, and expanded by Ken Andersen of Walter Andersen Nursery*

New content by Tom Spellman and Stark Brothers Nursery

Published by Walter Andersen Nursery
12755 Danielson Court
Poway, CA 92064-6847

©2020 Walter Andersen Nursery

ISBN: 978-0-615-54134-1

First Edition – January, 1944
Second Edition – February, 1944
Third Edition – October, 1944
Fourth Edition – November, 1945
Fifth Edition – October, 1946
Sixth Edition – October, 1947
Seventh Edition – March, 1950
Eighth – November, 1965
Ninth Edition – March, 1975
Tenth Edition – October, 1978
Eleventh Edition – November, 1980
Twelfth Edition – February, 1984
Thirteenth Edition – January, 1987
Fourteenth Edition – February, 1988
Fifteenth Edition – February, 1990
Sixteenth Edition – February, 1992
Seventeenth Edition – February, 1995
Eighteenth Edition – January, 1997
Nineteenth Edition – October, 1999
Twentieth Edition – September, 2001
Twenty-First Edition – September, 2011
Twenty-Second Edition – January, 2012
Twenty-Third Edition – November, 2012
Twenty-Fourth Edition – September, 2014
Twenty-Fifth Edition – April, 2018
Twenty-Sixth Edition – November, 2020

Table of Contents

Foreward

The subject covered in R. Sanford Martin's book is here largely as a result of many requests from those who used his first book, "How to Prune Western Shrubs." Martin hesitated in having this book printed because he was aware that this subject has been well covered many times by others, and in much greater detail. In recent years, the book had been out of print and as copies made their way into consumer's hands, it became more and more scarce, until I couldn't find any copies available for sale other than a few offered online. The number of requests I received for it, along with the usual 300 sold in our stores annually, convinced me that this book would continue to delight readers long after seeing print for the first time in 1944.

In re-publishing this book, I kept many of Martin's instructions as he wrote them. For each type of fruit tree discussed, Martin attempted to bring out the main reason why that particular tree needs pruning. To one who understands how, where, and why a tree bears fruit, pruning is an extremely simple job. I have attempted to modernize some of the language. There are some new chapters that include rose pruning. Some illustrations have been updated and photos have been added.

In keeping with Walter Andersen Nursery's history of primarily working with the home gardener, this book continues to be a reference guide for hobbyists and is not intended for the commercial orchardist.

In fact, in some cases, the procedure which Martin recommended is quite contrary to general orchard practice. The owner of a few trees for home consumption alone is not concerned with picking costs, maximum trees per acre, and mechanical cultivation problems. In many homes, the fruit trees are neglected because no experienced pruner is at hand at the time the pruning should be done, and again, the price paid to have one or two trees pruned is out of proportion to the amount of fruit harvested.

We are deeply grateful to Tom Spellman of Dave Wilson Nursery and Stark Brothers Nursery for allowing us to use their content in the new chapters of this book.

— Ken Andersen | *CEO, Walter Andersen Nursery*

Preface

New fruit gardeners will always have questions and concerns. Never be afraid to ask for help from veteran growers or your local retail nursery. That being said, the best way to accumulate experience and knowledge is to spend time with your trees. You will notice when trees begin to grow in the spring, when and where they bloom, how long the flowers take to set small fruit, and watch as the fruit progresses through the season. You will begin to identify if and when you have an insect or disease problem. Being observant of these issues is the key to success. See how the trees' growth slows in the fall. Enjoy the spectacular fall colors and the calm of the winter dormant season. Just like an old friend, the only way to get to know something or someone is to spend time with them. Spend some time with your trees.

— **Tom Spellman** | *Dave Wilson Nursery*

Backyard Orchard Culture

WHAT IS BACKYARD ORCHARD CULTURE?

The objective of Backyard Orchard Culture is a prolonged harvest of tree-ripe fruit from a small space in the yard. This is accomplished by planting an assortment of fruit trees close together and keeping them small by summer pruning.

Backyard Orchard Culture Is Not Commercial Orchard Culture

For years, most of the information about growing fruit came from commercial orchard culture: methods that promoted maximum size for maximum yield but required 12-foot ladders for pruning, thinning and picking, and 400 to 600 square feet of land per tree. Tree spacing had to allow for tractors.

Most people today do not need nor expect commercial results from their backyard fruit trees. A commercial grower would never consider using his methods on a 90 ft. x 100 ft. parcel, so why should a homeowner?

Backyard Orchard Culture Is High Density Planting and Successive Ripening

The length of the fruit season is maximized by planting several (or many) fruit varieties with different ripening times.

Because of the limited space available to most homeowners, this means using one or more of the techniques for close-planting and training fruit trees; two, three or four trees in one hole, espalier, and hedgerow are the most common of these techniques.

Four Trees Instead of One Means Ten to Twelve Weeks of Fruit Instead of Only Two or Three

Close-planting offers the additional advantage of restricting a tree's vigor. A tree won't grow as large when there are competing trees close by. Close-planting works best when rootstocks of similar vigor are planted together.

As a four-in-one-hole planting, for example, four trees on Citation rootstock would be easier to maintain than a combination of one tree on Lovell, one on Mazzard, one on Citation, and one on M-27.

In many climates, planting more varieties can also mean better cross-pollination of pears, apples, plums and cherries, which means more consistent production.

Backyard Orchard Culture Means Accepting the Responsibility for Tree Size

Small trees yield crops of manageable size and are much easier to spray, thin, prune, net and harvest than large trees.

If trees are kept small, it is possible to plant a greater number of trees in a given space, affording the opportunity for more kinds of fruit and a longer fruit season.

Most semi-dwarfing rootstocks do not control fruit tree size as much as most people expect.

Rootstocks can help to improve fruit tree soil and climate adaptation, pest and disease resistance, precocity (heavier bearing in early years), longevity, and ease of propagation in the nursery.

To date, no rootstocks have been developed which do all these things plus fully dwarf the grafted scion.

Pruning is the only way to keep most fruit trees under 12' tall.

The most practical method of pruning for size control is summer pruning.

Tree Size Is the Grower's Responsibility

Choose a size and don't let the tree get any bigger. A good height is the height you can reach for thinning and picking while standing on the ground or on a low stool.

Two other important influences on tree size are irrigation and fertilization practices. Fruit trees should not be grown with lots of nitrogen and lots of water. Some people grow their fruit trees the way they grow their lawn, then wonder why the trees are so big and don't have any fruit!

Backyard Orchard Culture Means Understanding the Reasons for Pruning

It's much easier to keep a small tree small than it is to make a large tree small.

Most kinds of deciduous fruit trees require pruning to stimulate new fruiting wood, remove broken and diseased wood, space the fruiting wood and allow good air circulation and sunlight penetration in the canopy.

Pruning is most important in the first three years, because this is when the shape and size of a fruit tree is established.

Pruning at the same time as thinning the crop is strongly recommended.

By pruning when there is fruit on the tree, the kind of wood on which the tree sets fruit (one year-old wood, two year-old wood, spurs, etc.) is apparent, which helps you to make better pruning decisions.

Backyard Orchard Culture Means Summer Pruning for Size Control

There are several reasons why summer pruning is the easiest way to keep fruit trees small. Reducing the canopy by pruning in summer reduces photosynthesis (food manufacture), thereby reducing the capacity for new growth. Summer pruning also reduces the total amount of food materials and energy available to be stored in the root system in late summer and fall. This controls vigor the following spring, since spring growth is supported primarily by stored foods and energy. Also, for many people, pruning is more enjoyable in nice weather than in winter, hence it is more likely to get done.

Backyard Orchard Culture Means Not Being Intimidated by Planting or Pruning

Fruit tree planting and pruning needn't be complicated nor confusing. When planting, be aware of air circulation. This is important for minimizing disease problems. Check drainage. If poor-draining soil is suspected, consider a raised bed to protect the roots from starving for oxygen when the soil is water-logged. Up to four trees can be planted in a 4x4 foot bed raised at least 12 inches above the surrounding soil. For more trees, shape a larger bed to fit the available space.

Pruning in Backyard Orchard Culture is simple. When planting a bareroot tree, cut side limbs back by at least two-thirds to promote vigorous new growth.

FIRST YEAR

At planting time, bareroot trees may be topped as low as 15 inches above the ground to force very low scaffold limbs or, alternatively, trees may be topped higher than 15 inches (up to four feet) depending on the presence of well-spaced side limbs or desired tree form. After the spring flush of growth, cut the new growth back by half (late April/early May in central Calif.). In late summer (late August to mid-September), cut the subsequent growth back by half. Size control and development of low fruiting wood begin in the first year. Note, two year old trees or fruit trees established in containers should not be pruned back as far as first year trees. Two year old and established containerized trees should only be cut back to the top of the scaffolding.

When selecting containerized trees for planting in late spring/early summer, select trees with well-placed low scaffold limbs.

These are usually trees that were cut back when potted to force low growth. Cut back new growth by half now, and again in late summer.

Two, Three or Four Trees in One Hole

At planting time, plant each tree 18 to 24 inches apart. Cut back all trees to the same height.

Cut back new growth by half in spring and late summer as above. Especially in the first two years, cut back vigorous varieties as often as necessary to keep them in proportion (very important!).

Do not allow any variety to dominate and shade out the others.

Plant each grouping of three or four trees in one hole at least 18 inches apart (between closest trees) to allow for adequate light penetration and good air circulation.

Hedgerow plantings: easiest to maintain when spaced at least three feet apart. Make sure the placement of the hedgerow does not block air circulation and light for other plantings.

To conserve water and stabilize soil moisture, apply at least a four-inch layer of mulch up to four feet from a single tree or from the center of a two-, three-, or four-trees-in-one-hole planting.

SECOND YEAR

Cut back new growth by half in spring and late summer, same as the first year.

Pruning three times may be the easiest way to manage some vigorous varieties: spring, early summer and late summer.

Single-tree plantings: prune to vase shape (open center, no central leader). For multi-plantings: thin out the center to allow plenty of sunlight into the interior of the group of trees.

Remove broken limbs. Remove diseased limbs well below signs of disease.

THIRD YEAR

Choose a height and don't let the tree grow any taller.

Tree height is the decision of the pruner. Whenever there are vigorous shoots above the chosen height, cut back or remove them. Each year, in late spring/early summer, cut back all new growth by at least half.

The smaller one-, two-, and three-year-old branches that bear the fruit should have at least six inches of free space all around. This means that where two branches begin close together and grow in the same direction, one should be removed.

When limbs cross one another, one or both should be cut back or removed.

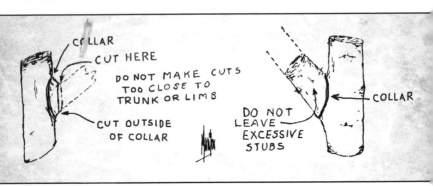

When removing large limbs, first saw part way through the limb on the under side ahead of your intended cut. Do this so it won't tear the trunk as it comes off. Also, don't make the final cut flush with the trunk or parent limb; be sure to leave a collar (a short stub).

Apricots will require more pruning in the summer to control height. Prune as needed (two to three times in the summer) to remove excessive growth. Be careful not to cut too much at one time, as this might cause excess sun exposure and sunburn to the unprotected interior limbs.

To develop an espalier, fan, or other two-dimensional form, simply remove everything that doesn't grow flat. Selectively thin and train what's left to space the fruiting wood.

Don't let pruning decisions inhibit you or slow you down. There are always multiple acceptable decisions—no two people will prune a tree in the same way. You learn to prune by pruning!

Backyard Orchard Culture Begins with Summer Pruning

Smaller trees are easier to spray, prune, thin, net and harvest! With small trees, it's possible to have more varieties that ripen at different times. The easiest way to keep trees small is by summer pruning. There are lots of styles, methods and techniques of summer pruning. The important thing is to prune!

Backyard Orchard Culture Is the Pride of Accomplishment

A definite sense of accomplishment and satisfaction is derived from growing your own fruit. There is pleasure in growing new varieties, in producing fruit that is unusually sweet and tasty, in providing an assortment of fruit over a months-long season, and in sharing tree-ripe fruit with others. These are the rewards of learning and experimenting with new cultural practices and techniques as you become an accomplished backyard fruit grower.

Backyard Orchard Culture Means Knowing Your Nursery Professional

The concepts and techniques of Backyard Orchard Culture are learned and implemented year by year. An integral part of Backyard Orchard Culture is knowing your nursery professionals and consulting them when you have questions.

ULTIMUS DICTUM

There's no excuse for neglected trees, maintenance undone or lack of know-how. Backyard Orchard Culture is an attitude: Just Do It!

Planting Your Backyard Orchard

KNOW YOUR SITE'S DRAINAGE

Most fruit trees will not survive in soil that drains so slowly it remains water-saturated for extended periods. Before planting, be sure you are familiar with how well your soil drains.

Test Your Drainage

- Dig a hole about 1 foot deep and fill it with water.

- If the water drains within three or four hours, fill the hole again.

- If it takes longer than three or four hours to drain on the 1st or 2nd filling, you have problems!

If Your Intended Planting Site Drains Poorly:

- Don't plant there.

- Plant the tree above the present soil line by constructing a berm, mound or raised bed.

- Install a French Drain (a trench filled with gravel or rock that allows water to drain away from the planting area

Berms and Mounds

The root crown, the upper part of the root system to just below the soil line, is the most vulnerable part of a tree. In many instances, a 6-12" high raised planting area (mound or berm) is sufficient to raise tree root crowns above wet soil. A six inch high mound should be at least 2 1/2 feet in diameter, a 10- to 12-inch mound or berm at least three to four feet wide. Mounds should have as gentle a slope as possible to minimize erosion.

Raised Bed

A good way to plant trees higher than the surrounding soil is to make a bottomless box using 2x12 redwood or cedar or other material such as rock or concrete block.

Sun

For the healthiest trees and tastiest fruit, choose the sunniest available planting location. The main exception is a low desert climate where summer temperatures reach 110°+. Fruit trees there benefit from some afternoon shade.

Layout and Spacing

Spacing depends on your objectives, your plan—how much fruit you want from each tree, how many trees are wanted in the total space available and how you intend to control tree size. (Remember, small trees maintained by summer pruning are much easier to spray, thin, prune and harvest than large trees.)

If using high density planting techniques, plant as close as 18 inches apart for 2, 3 or 4 trees in one hole and 2 or 3 feet apart for a hedgerow.

If you have plenty of space and want larger trees, plant at wider spacing. It's up to you.

Reminder: If multi-planting, plant trees with similar rootstocks and trees with similar spray requirements together. Contact the local nursery professional in your area for spray recommendations.

ABOUT PLANTING FRUIT TREES

Fertilizer

Properly done, mixing an organic starter fertilizer with the soil at the bottom of your planting hole will boost your trees vigor and growth.

Soil Amendments

Adding organic matter to well-draining soil can help retain moisture in the root zone of newly planted trees, and as it decomposes, enhances your soil. Check with your nursery professional regarding recommended soil amendments. Ultimately, trees must grow in the surrounding soil, so don't make a hole of amended soil surrounded by slow-draining native soil. The tree hole will just fill with water, killing the tree. The only remedy for poorly draining soil is some sort of raised bed or planting in containers.

Planting Depth

When planted, the tree should be at the height it was in the nursery; the nursery soil line is visible on the trunk as a slight change in bark color. It's very important not to plant the tree too low. If you will be watering the tree after planting (as you should when planting in fast-draining soil), plant an inch or two high to allow for settling.

Caring For Bare Root Trees

Bare root trees should be planted as soon as possible after purchasing. If buying trees before planting day, keep the roots wrapped or covered to maintain moisture and high humidity, and store in a cool location. Bare root trees may be kept before planting by heeling in: cover the roots with a moist (not soggy) medium such as sawdust, sand or porous soil. Do not let the roots dry out or freeze. Do not use sawdust as a soil amendment when planting.

HOW TO PLANT A FRUIT TREE

Dig the hole a little deeper than the root is tall—and make it wide enough to accommodate the longest roots without bending.

- Loosen the sides of the hole. Roots sometimes do not readily penetrate a slick interface.

• Backfill with amended soil until the bottom of the hole is at the right planting depth for the tree, and tamp. If multi-planting in one hole, backfill to correct planting depth for each tree.

• Prune off any broken, rotted or twisted roots, making a clean cut.

• Position the tree, spread the roots and refill the hole, tamping the soil around the roots as you go.

• If planting in fast-draining soil, water thoroughly in order to finish settling the soil around the roots. In slower-draining soils, water a little at a time, over several days if necessary.

• Usually, no further water is necessary until there is new growth of several inches.

Note: If there is a prevailing wind in your area that reaches your site, compensate by leaning the tree slightly into the upwind direction when you plant. The side of the tree where the grafted scion emerges from the rootstock should be pointing upwind.

PLANTING IN A RAISED BED

Construct a three to four foot square box for a single tree, 5 ft. x 5 ft. for four trees in one planter.

• Place the box on the poorly draining spot.

• Dig a shallow hole only if necessary to allow for proper planting depth (see above). In any viable garden soil, tree roots will find their own way to anchorage.

• Place the tree in the box, spread the roots and fill the box with soil (slightly amended if necessary), tamping the soil around the roots as you go.

• Water as needed to maintain soil moisture around the roots.

LAST STEPS

Pruning

If you want the fruiting wood to begin low, smaller trees may be cut back at planting time to a height as low as the knee (15-20 inches). Any remaining side limbs should be cut back to one or two buds. Larger trees may be cut above existing well-placed low limbs, or they too may be cut back low to force new, lower limbs. Remember, not to cut back established trees down to the main trunk. Many varieties once established two years or more or in containers, especially peach and nectarine have blind eye buds on the main trunk and won't produce re-growth except from scaffold. Work with the lowest scaffold branching and cut it back to two or three buds from the trunk.

Paint the Trunk

Sunburn can damage newly planted trees, especially in the climates of the southwestern U.S. An interior white latex paint diluted 50% with water, can help protect trees from this problem. Paint your newly-planted trees from the ground all the way to the top.

Mulch!

Mulch applied as a top dressing is beneficial to plants and the soil, as mulch decomposes it provides a steady source of nutrients to plants and organic matter to the soil. It also helps to stabilize and conserve soil moisture.

Water and Mulch

HOW MUCH WATER? WHY MULCH?

For the longest time, gardeners and nursery folks have dealt with the water problem. It's common to wonder why a plant is dying when it is given plenty of water.

As all accomplished gardeners know, "plenty of water" can easily be too much water for many plants, especially in slow-draining soils.

How Much Water?

A poor understanding of how to water a plant, giving too much or too little, is the most common reason why novice gardeners lose plants. Too often, their remedy for a drooping plant is more fertilizer and more water when, in fact, what the plant needs is less water.

Of course, in sandy, fast-draining soils, neglecting to water, especially during a hot spell, can quickly do irreparable damage to a plant. That's an easy lesson to learn.

In clay soils or any poorly-draining soil, the opposite is true. The damage is done by too much water, primarily by denying oxygen to the roots. Plants may decline slowly or suddenly. Fruit trees in wet soils may struggle for years and never perform as they should. In addition, trees stressed by lack of oxygen in the root zone are more susceptible to disease and insect damage.

For any soil, a drip system is an effective and water-efficient way to irrigate fruit trees. Use sufficient emitters to wet the entire area under the canopy to a depth of at least two feet.

Check Your Soil Moisture

Get acquainted with your soil and drainage. Your surface soil moisture might be wetter or drier—from the soil a foot or more deep.

Periodically, including during a hot spell and a few days after a heavy rain or watering, dig to a depth of a foot or so and actually observe and feel the soil moisture. After you've done this a few times, you will begin to develop an instinct as to when your soil is wet and when it is about to become dry. This can also be accomplished with a moisture meter. Make sure when using the meter that you insert it to a consistent depth beneath the soil surface. You can mark the probe with a piece of electrical tape at the depth you want to use. Once you get the trees acclimated to the watering schedule you have set observations of meter readings that provide an indication of when additional irrigation may be needed.

Examining your trees and other plants as you observe soil moisture will soon give you above-ground indicators. Staying in touch with your soil moisture as the weather fluctuates is an important part of gardening.

Mulch

So what does the drooping plant need? For any soil, fast draining or slow, steady soil moisture and nutrient supply go a long way toward establishing a lush, healthy garden for both fruiting and ornamental plants. An often over-looked means of achieving that is mulching the soil surface.

What's the deal with mulch? Mulch is good for the soil and the plants, conserving water, and minimizing the use of synthetic fertilizers. A 2" to 6" layer of bio diverse mulch will provide the following:

• Make better use of irrigation by up to 50%.

• Reduce summer soil surface temperatures by 10° to 20°F.

- Encourage establishment of important mycorrhizal fungi that allow plants to take up nutrients in an efficient and natural manner.

- Stops germination of 80% or more of weed seeds. Do not mulch over Bermuda or rhizomatous grasses. Control the grass before mulching.

Mulch, for Our Purposes, Is Compost That Includes Larger Particles

The use of mulch as a top dressing is an effective way of cutting down water requirements. Covering the surface of the soil with mulch lessens the evaporation. The root zone stays cool, which also cuts down evaporation and extends the time between watering.

In slow-draining soils, mulch covering the surface gives water more time to penetrate the entire root zone before the top layer becomes dry. In all soils, consistent moisture and a cool root zone reduces stress to plants during hot weather.

Mulch, as it decomposes, provides a steady source of nutrients to the plants, thereby cutting down the need for and overuse of fertilizers.

As it decomposes, mulch provides the soil with organic matter, which is an essential component of all good garden soils.

Mulch is simple to apply and simple to maintain. You'll find mulch at your local nursery or call around your hometown. Many cities sell mulch very cheaply or even give it away (they haul all those leaves off the streets and parks and put them somewhere to begin composting).

Don't forget that you can make your own mulch! There are many different materials for the home gardener and many different web sites to find the one right for you. To make your mulch look pretty, you can use a top dressing such as bark (small preferred) straw, alfalfa hay, cocoa bean hulls, wood chips, and oak leaves. You can find top dressing packaged in bags at your local retailer.

Mulch is good for the environment. By using mulch, you help cut down on the waste going into landfills. With the concern over nitrates in the ground and water, the use of mulches prepares us for a future when high nitrogen fertilizers are not encouraged. There is not a lot of nitrogen in mulch, and what is there is recycled by the plants rather than finding its way into our water systems.

Finally, and maybe most importantly, is the need for water conservation. Availability of water for a growing population is more problematic year by year. In order to maintain our gardening lifestyle for decades to come, we all must become aware of how to use water more effectively. Part of the solution is mulch.

Where is the Fruit?

TWO COMMONLY FRUSTRATING QUESTIONS ANY GROWER MIGHT ASK:

"Why won't my fruit tree bloom?"

"Why doesn't my tree have fruit?"

You've planted your fruit tree. It's growing. It's living. But it's not blooming or bearing fruit. While this can be discouraging to the point of wanting to chop the tree down, go for the facts—not the axe. Your fruit tree may not bloom or bear for a number of reasons. In this chapter, we focus on the 6 basic requirements of fruit trees and address the most common issues and solutions related to fruit production.

6 BASIC NEEDS FOR FRUIT PRODUCTION

1. Tree Development

If your fruit tree is still too young/immature, it won't go into fruit-production mode. When you purchase bare root fruit trees, they will be around 2 years old and will still need a few years before reaching their fruiting maturity. For more information about how long it takes for different trees to bear, refer to the following chart before deciding your tree has an issue.

"Years to Fruit" begins counting after the trees are transplanted into your growing space. *(see chart on page 24.)*

For colder-zoned folks, citrus trees can be grown in containers and brought inside over the winter. Hitting the top of the waiting list are sweet cherries and pawpaws. These edibles require a longer-term commitment, so it's best to get these started right away so that you can enjoy the edibles you love as soon as possible! While they're growing, these trees make for some beautiful landscape additions.

YEARS TO FRUIT

FRUIT TREE TYPE	YEARS TO FRUIT
Apple Trees	2-3 years
Apricot Trees	2-3 years
Cherry Trees (sour)	2-3 years
Cherry Trees (sweet)	2-3 years
Citrus Trees	2-3 years
Fig Trees	1-2 years
Mulberry Trees	1-2 years
Nectarine Trees	1-2 years
Peach Trees	1-2 years
Pear Trees	2-3 years
Persimmon Trees	2-3 years
Plum Trees	2-3 years
Pomegranate Trees	2-3 years

2. Pollination
Fruit trees require pollination to set fruit. If your tree is not self-pollinating, it needs a compatible pollinator tree planted nearby, generally within 50 feet. Also, pollination-helping beneficials like bees, birds, and wind need to be adequately present. If your tree is missing these important elements, even though it may bloom, it may not set fruit.

3. Chill Hours
Trees should be hardy to your zone for a chance to survive winters and summers.

Trees should receive adequate chill hours to produce fruit. Chill hours are based on temperatures that stay below 45°F during the tree's dormant period. If the tree is hardy to your zone but does not meet its chill-hour requirement, its fruit production will decrease. However, now you can usually find a high or low chill variety of most types of fruit that will suit your growing conditions.

Weather can greatly affect fruit production. If a late frost zaps your tree's blossoms or young fruit, then it will not be able to produce a crop for you to harvest that year. If a drought or intense heat/cold damages your trees and their buds, you simply have to care for your trees this year (as usual) and wait for more favorable weather next year. Also, drought stress during the previous summer flower bud forming period will prevent bloom the following year.

4. Pruning
Regularly pruned trees are much more apt to produce quality fruit. Fruiting buds tend to form on limbs that have adequate air circulation and light infiltration, which is your goal when pruning. Learn about pruning later in this book.

You also have to make sure that you find the right balance for pruning. Heavy, over-pruning can cause a tree to produce too much vegetative growth in response, and under-pruning can contribute to the development of too much fruiting wood, which is the culprit for overbearing, small fruit, and fruit drop. Remember to thin young fruit to develop the best quality fruit.

5. Spacing
Fruit trees that are planted too close to one another will compete for nutrients and light. If planting trees close together is part of your design (espalier and high-density plantings are two prime examples), then you will need to prune accordingly to keep them open to light and ensure the trees are getting enough nutrients from the soil.

If trees are planted too close to buildings and other structures, they will have similar conflicts with the added risk of interfering with those structures. Make sure you give your trees enough room to grow and flourish.

6. Soil Conditions

It is very important that your trees have the right balance of stored energy and soil nutrients. This is the best thing you can do to ensure your tree fruits and has energy to support its fruit. If this balance is off, it can have a negative impact on how your tree blooms or bears.

If a tree has plenty of stored energy but a shortage of soil nutrients, you may see a stunted crop of undersized, poor-quality fruit. You might even see no fruit at all. This can happen if your tree has tried to overbear, which may cause a tree to drop its fruit prematurely. It may also happen if your tree has experienced foliage-depletion, which can be caused by stress, weather, or other weakening factors (animals, pests, or disease). Identifying the stress factor and treating it will help to remedy the problem. You can have your soil tested to find nutrient deficiencies. You should implement routine control of pests and disease.

A tree can also have an excess of soil nutrients but not enough stored energy. The tree will appear to be healthy and lush during the growing season, but it will not bear fruit (regardless of maturity) since, in many cases, the tree doesn't even bloom. This happens as a result of "over-feeding". If the soil provides plenty of nutrients, like nitrogen (either naturally or by adding fertilizer), the tree develops an excess of vegetative growth that will delay the growth of fruiting buds. You can remedy this problem by holding off on fertilizing or using a fertilizer with low nitrogen but moderate phosphorus and potash like a 3-12-12.

DESPERATE TIMES CALL FOR DESPERATE MEASURES

There is an extreme solution that should only be attempted if all else fails: root-pruning your trees.

Root Pruning

Bring a spade or shovel out to the drip line of your trees. The drip line is where the tips of the branches are, but straight down on the ground. Take the spade or shovel and push it straight into the ground and pull it straight back out. Do not dig out any dirt. Move over a foot or two and repeat the process. You are essentially creating a dotted-line circle around your tree's root system, which will clip the feeder roots and "shock" the tree into blooming during the next growing season.

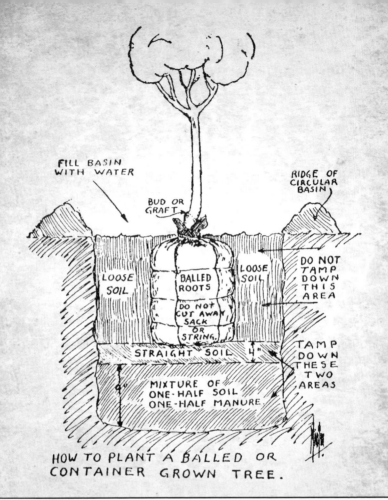

FILL BASIN WITH WATER

RIDGE OF CIRCULAR BASIN

BUD OR GRAFT

DO NOT TAMP DOWN THIS AREA

LOOSE SOIL

BALLED ROOTS

LOOSE SOIL

DO NOT CUT AWAY SACK OR STRING.

STRAIGHT SOIL 4"

TAMP DOWN THESE TWO AREAS

MIXTURE OF ONE-HALF SOIL ONE-HALF MANURE

HOW TO PLANT A BALLED OR CONTAINER GROWN TREE.

Planting Young Trees

EDITOR'S NOTE

When reading this chapter, bear in mind that the illustrations used are the original to the book. Planting theory and practice has changed over the decades since the original edition was published in 1944. Rather than re-illustrate these images we have updated the text in the chapter to be in line with current planting theory. Since balled and burlaped trees are rarely seen in the fruit tree business the chapter on balled and container trees will refer only to container trees. The planting of balled trees, should in the rare instance you find one, would follow the same parameters as a container tree.

BARE-ROOT OR TREES IN CONTAINERS

Dig holes at least half again as wide as the diameter of the container. The depth of the hole should be such that when the root ball is set into it, the bud or graft is slightly above the surrounding soil level. In the original illustration, this would mean a depth to the top of the STRAIGHT SOIL line shown. Carefully remove the tree from the container and set the root ball on top of the soil upright in the center of the hole. Fill in the remainder of the hole with amended soil lightly tamping it down as you fill. Ask your local nursery or garden center what soil amendment they recommend when planting fruit trees. When filled in, build a basin for holding water by creating a berm around the perimeter of the hole.

Allow water to slowly fill in the basin. By allowing the water to help settle the soil around the root ball there will be no air pockets where the new roots will develop. Water as required by your particular soil conditions.

BARE-ROOT TREES

Dig holes at least half again as wide as the widest spread of the roots. The depth of the hole should be measured so that the bud or graft is above the surrounding soil level. In the original illustration this would mean a depth to the top of the STRAIGHT SOIL line shown. Carefully spread the roots on top of the soil with the trunk upright in the center of the hole. Start filling the hole lightly with amended soil taking care to cover all of the roots, lightly tamping it down as you go to eliminate air pockets. Once roots are covered, fill in

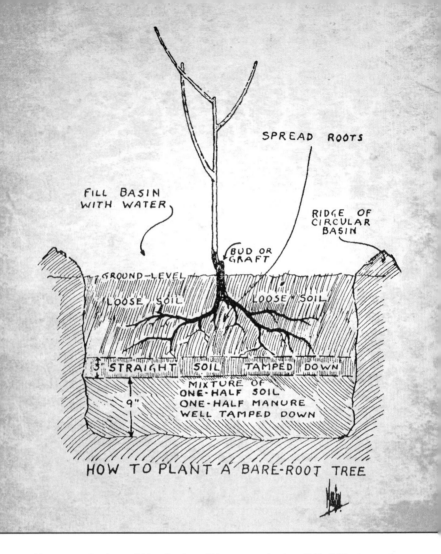

SPREAD ROOTS

FILL BASIN
WITH WATER

RIDGE OF
CIRCULAR
BASIN

BUD OR
GRAFT

GROUND-LEVEL

LOOSE SOIL   LOOSE SOIL

3" STRAIGHT SOIL TAMPED DOWN

MIXTURE OF
ONE-HALF SOIL
9"   ONE-HALF MANURE
WELL TAMPED DOWN

HOW TO PLANT A BARE-ROOT TREE

the remainder of the hole with amended soil lightly tamping it down. Ask your local nursery or garden center what soil amendment they recommend when planting fruit trees. When filled in, build a basin for holding water by creating a berm around the perimeter of the hole.

Allow water to slowly fill in the basin. By allowing the water to help settle the soil around the root ball there will be no air pockets where the new roots will develop. Water as required by your particular soil conditions. If the soil settles and exposes roots, sink them back into the soil and cover them with more soil.

Trees should be planted at the same depth they were grown in the ground, usually about an inch or two above the upper most roots below the graft or bud. Sometimes you can see where the existing soil level was on the bark of the tree. If you are not sure, ask your nursery or garden center associate to show you where the soil level should be on your trees. It is most important to make sure that you do not plant the trees any deeper than they had been grown at the nursery of origin.

Planting Tips

- Keep the soil around the roots of fruit trees at as even a moisture content as possible. Irrigate as often as necessary, according to your soil, depending on soil type, rain, temperature, etc.

- Add mulch under a tree; this will help to preserve the moisture and prevent the surface from baking, and as mulch breaks down it enhances the soil.

- Always cultivate to the same depth. This keeps the feeder roots at one depth, and they will not be damaged by too deep a cultivation.

- Never spray fruit trees while they are in full bloom as this will ruin the flower pollination and no fruit will set.

- In the average soil, one surface inch of water will penetrate to about one foot of depth, furnishing adequate moisture. Two inches of water to a two foot depth, etc. Keep the moisture content of your soil as near constant as possible.

- Any soil requires a constant addition of organic matter, as well as fertilizer, to keep it from baking hard and to keep the essential soil organisms alive.

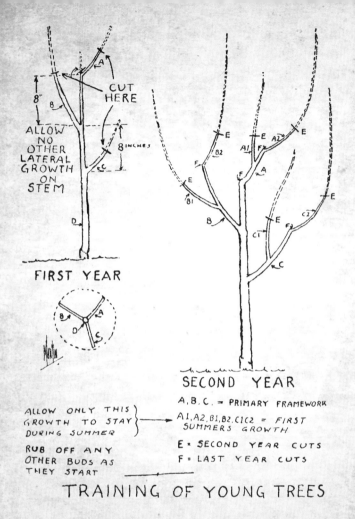

CUT HERE

8"

8

ALLOW NO OTHER LATERAL GROWTH ON STEM

8 INCHES

D

FIRST YEAR

SECOND YEAR

A, B, C. = PRIMARY FRAMEWORK

A1, A2, B1, B2, C1 C2 = FIRST SUMMERS GROWTH

E = SECOND YEAR CUTS

F = LAST YEAR CUTS

ALLOW ONLY THIS GROWTH TO STAY DURING SUMMER

RUB OFF ANY OTHER BUDS AS THEY START

TRAINING OF YOUNG TREES

Training of Young Trees

The success of any fruit tree, particularly the deciduous types, depends a great deal upon the training it receives during the first three years after being planted. These instructions will apply to any type of deciduous tree, with the exception of Walnuts and Pecans.

FIRST YEAR

Let it be assumed that the fruit tree has been purchased from the nursery and is already planted in the ground according to the "Planting Instructions" as given earlier in this book.

Cut off the main leader or central stem, at about 30 inches from the ground. If there are any lateral branches on the tree, make this cut immediately above a good strong lateral branch at about the height mentioned above.

Then select two other lateral branches, if other than a whip growth, one about 8 inches below the top one, and another about 16 inches below the top. Make your selection of these branches so that when you look straight down above the center the three branches trisect about equally, an imaginary circle drawn around the stem. See illustration.

Next, head these three lateral branches back to about one-half their total length. These three branches are the framework of the future tree and by selecting them spaced in the above manner, the tree will develop a crotch that is less apt to split in later years.

As the tree grows, allow only two buds to develop branches on each of the framework branches; one at the end, and one about halfway between the end and the base. Let these branches grow to the full development without further summer pruning and rub off any shoots that may appear on the trunk as suckers.

SECOND YEAR

There should now be six well developed branches on the young tree. Cut back these branches about two-thirds of their length. Cut just above a strong bud or lateral branch. Head back the lateral branches one-half their length.

The tree is now ready to produce fruit and the system of pruning that is recommended for the particular variety should be carried out.

All of this pruning should be done during the winter while tree is dormant, except where summer cutting is specified.

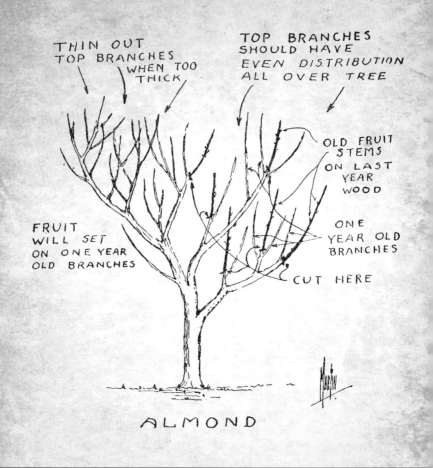

THIN OUT TOP BRANCHES WHEN TOO THICK

TOP BRANCHES SHOULD HAVE EVEN DISTRIBUTION ALL OVER TREE

OLD FRUIT STEMS ON LAST YEAR WOOD

ONE YEAR OLD BRANCHES

FRUIT WILL SET ON ONE YEAR OLD BRANCHES

CUT HERE

ALMOND

Almond

Almonds and Peaches are of the same family, but the Almond develops more erect growth, so it must be kept thinned out more carefully. The method of fruit production is also slightly different, so that heading back of the fruit-bearing wood is unnecessary as is the case with Peaches.

Pruning should be done during the winter months while the tree is dormant.

In some areas of the country there will be more die-back than in other areas. The first procedure is to remove any dead wood which has shown up during the past season. Second, cut out the least important of interfering or rubbing branches.

Fruit will be borne on an Almond tree on the one-year branches. Those are branches which grew during the last season's growing period will produce fruit this summer.

Prune out the twigs which produced fruit the last summer, leaving one or two new shoots which should have grown from near the base of the last year's fruiting wood. Make the cut immediately above the upper shoot to be left. These shoots or twigs, which remain, will be the best fruit producing wood. When this phase of the pruning is complete, the tree should have an even distribution of young branches all over the tree. If they are thicker in one portion of the tree top than another, do a little further thinning until the distribution of one-year branches is even.

Because of the brittle characteristic of Almond wood, it is desirable to encourage the growth to be erect, with the center of the tree well filled in.

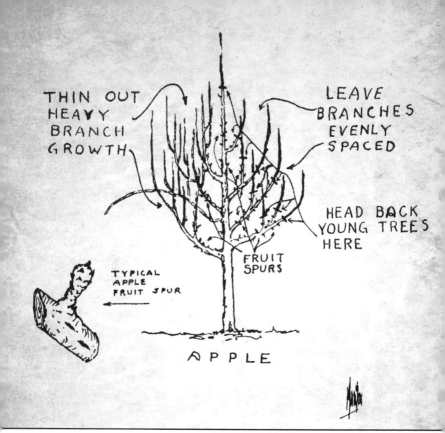

THIN OUT HEAVY BRANCH GROWTH

LEAVE BRANCHES EVENLY SPACED

HEAD BACK YOUNG TREES HERE

FRUIT SPURS

TYPICAL APPLE FRUIT SPUR

APPLE

Apple

There is no set habit of a bearing Apple tree, because, depending upon variety, the younger trees will vary from growing erect and slender to open and spreading. Eventually as the tree matures, it will develop into a fine spreading type. Observe your particular tree and if it is of the narrow erect type, according to its initial growth, make your pruning cuts just above buds which are pointed away from the center of the tree. If your variety of Apple is of the spreading type, make the cuts above buds pointed toward the center of the tree. The time for pruning is during the winter months.

All Apples produce their fruit on "spurs," which are formed on the branches one year old or more, usually in the lower portion of these branches. These "spurs" are developed from the short lateral growths that vary in length from one to three inches. After they have definitely formed they can be recognized by their thick stubby appearance. The spurs produce blossoms and fruit year after year, and should be saved wherever possible.

When pruning the Apple tree, first cut out any dead or diseased branches, being careful to make cuts close to the main branch, without leaving any stub. This is very important because all apples are quite susceptible to rot, which can easily start in a stub which is left long enough to die back, rather than heal over with bark and new wood growth.

Second, cut away any interfering wood, or branches that are rubbing against one another, or that have come down too close to the ground and hinder cultivation.

Third, cut out sufficient of the last year's branch growth to evenly space all branches, allowing even sunlight penetration throughout the tree top. In doing this cutting, be careful to leave all established fruit spurs and those small lateral bud developments that are to be future fruit spurs.

If the tree is making a normally rapid growth, especially a young tree, the new branch growth must be cut off just above the fruit spur buds. In the case of young trees, this will mean about two-thirds their length, as shown in the illustration.

Water sprouts or suckers should be cut out at any time that it is proven by their growth to be such. A sucker is a rapid growing shoot that comes from below the graft, and they should be removed as soon as they appear, by digging down to their base and cutting them off very close to the root or trunk. Water sprouts are "above ground suckers" and are recognized by their habit of growth, which is excessive in comparison with the rest of the branch growth of the tree. This growth is by nature, weak in structure and will not develop into suitable fruit producing wood, so cut it off clean and allow its sap to flow into more useful branches. These water sprouts, where allowed to grow will deprive the tree of valuable energy.

In the case of old trees which have lost a main branch or become one-sided, the water sprouts may be utilized to fill in vacant spaces, by heading them back, thereby forcing them to branch out and slow down their excessive soft growth.

Thinning the crop of fruit is frequently necessary with Apples, and this work should be done after the "June drop" has taken place. The "June drop" is a natural process with all fruit trees in an effort by nature to adjust the crop to what the tree can bear. This period is apt to occur any time after the first of May, to July, and if in your opinion there still remains too much fruit for your trees to ripen, they may be hand thinned, leaving the remaining fruit evenly spaced throughout the tree's branches.

As the Apple tree ages, there will be less and less pruning required. Give the tree its proper training in the first few years of its growth and this will insure less care as it grows older.

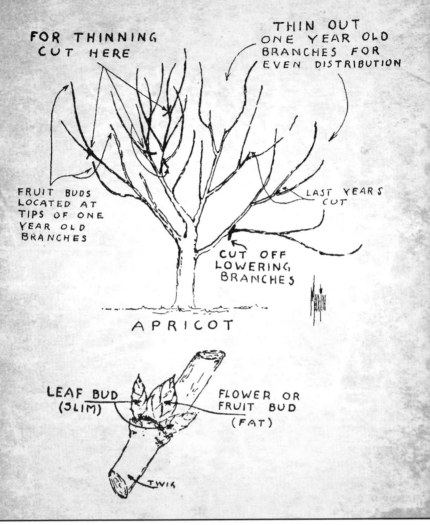

FOR THINNING
CUT HERE

THIN OUT
ONE YEAR OLD
BRANCHES FOR
EVEN DISTRIBUTION

FRUIT BUDS
LOCATED AT
TIPS OF ONE
YEAR OLD
BRANCHES

LAST YEARS
CUT

CUT OFF
LOWERING
BRANCHES

APRICOT

LEAF BUD
(SLIM)

FLOWER OR
FRUIT BUD
(FAT)

TWIG

Apricot

Like all other types of deciduous trees, the Apricot should be pruned during the dormant period or winter months, while the sap is inactive and the leaves are off the branches.

Apricots may be divided into three classes according to their fruit producing habits. In all cases the majority of the fruit is borne on one year old wood. Fruit may appear towards the tips of this growth, in the central section or in the lower section, and the fruiting habit of your tree may be ascertained by noting where the fattest buds are located on the one year old branches. The fattest or fullest buds are the flower producing buds, and indicate where the fruit will be set. The more slender buds will produce leaves and branch growth only.

In the case of the fruit buds being borne on the tip section, as is found in the "Royal" variety, do not head back the one year branches. In the case of the best fruit buds being in the central section, the one year growth may be headed back about one-third, and in the case of the fruit buds being in the lower branch section, the one year wood may be headed back from one-half to two-thirds of their length. The first type will apply in most cases, and in the event you cannot determine in which class your tree belongs it would be advisable to prune your tree as though it were of the first type and do not head back the one year branches.

All varieties of Apricots maintain the same general habit of tree growth and the same pruning rules apply to all of them. Prune out enough branches to evenly shape the top, selecting old wood wherever possible, and in doing this so space the branch growth to allow even sunlight penetration to all parts of the fruit producing top. The long whip-like branches which grew during last summer are the fruit producing wood for the coming year, so don't cut them too freely, and do not head back any of these branches unless the tree is of the second or third class as described.

The outside branches of the Apricot have a tendency to gradually lower each year, with the weight of fruit and foliage, and as these branches get low enough to interfere with cultivation, etc., they may be cut off without any damage to the tree. The nature of the tree is to replace these lowering outside branches with inside central growth, and these growths should be cared for as part of the original tree, and their development encouraged.

For the first four or five years of an Apricot tree's growth, its development is very rapid, and therefore their training is most important. Read the chapter on Training of Young Trees, and tend your trees accordingly.

Some varieties of Apricots will develop fruit spurs on the older wood, and wherever they appear they should be left because their fruit is always strong and well developed.

Because the Apricot wood is brittle, care should be taken not to allow any one branch or branches to spread laterally too great a distance. This practice encourages breakage of limbs. Favor erect growth wherever possible. A sturdy framework on your tree is desirable, even at the expense of early fruit production. A well spaced, husky framework of branches will have fewer tendencies to break under an abnormally heavy crop, than a tree that has been allowed to grow undirected.

AVOCADO

Avocado

There is no fruit grown which has developed more different schools of thought regarding correct pruning, than has the Avocado. R. Sanford Martin witnessed the practice and results of various methods used in commercial plantings of this fruit, and when they are consistently carried out, give satisfactory results as far as fruit production and harvesting is concerned. However, as this book is devoted to the production of fruit on a small scale such as the average home with one or more Avocado trees, instructions shall be confined to methods believed most practical to this small scale production, where economy of harvesting is not an item to be considered.

One of the first things to be remembered with Avocados is that in its natural habitat the tree grows in semi-tropical forests and, therefore, the more nearly we can reproduce such a growing condition the more success we shall have.

First, because of their natural home being in forests, the trees have developed the characteristic of the feeding roots being very close to the surface of the ground, which in the forest would be covered by a thick carpet of fallen leaves. Therefore, reproduce this condition as nearly as possible with good quality mulch, but never allow grass to grow over the roots.

Second, natural forests are not cultivated; hence the feeder roots are close to the surface. Cultivation renders surface roots useless, which frequently results in the dropping of fruit in any stage of development. Consequently, mulch your Avocado trees well and don't cultivate.

As far as fruit production is concerned, the Avocado needs no pruning, but because of the weak nature of branch wood, and heavy leaves and fruit, the outer branches will constantly be lowering year after year until they are touching the ground. These lower branches should be removed gradually so as not to produce a "hole" in the tree's foliage which might allow sunburn of the inner branch bark.

It is the nature of the primary or bright green bark on the main trunk and branches to sunburn unless well protected by the foliage. This sunburn hardens the bark and slows down the sap activity to such an extent that it makes a difficult condition to overcome without expert attention. In young trees where a main branch or stem has become sunburned from exposure, try to encourage a new branch from below the affected area to grow in place of the sunburned branch.

If your tree grows one-sided, as is frequently the case with backyard Avocados, head back the tip growth gradually, on the heavy side of the tree, thereby forcing growth in other portions. As your trees reach mature growth their one-sidedness will be eliminated naturally.

Pruning may be done whenever lowering branches make it necessary. Die-back branches on the inside of the tree should be cut out as they appear. The older the tree, the less trimming will be needed.

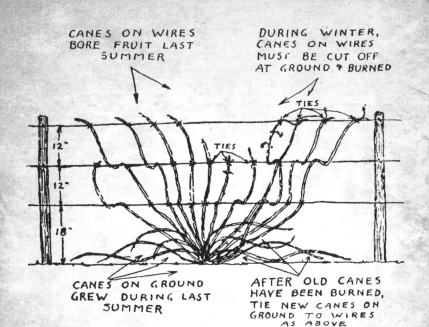

CANES ON WIRES
BORE FRUIT LAST
SUMMER

DURING WINTER,
CANES ON WIRES
MUST BE CUT OFF
AT GROUND & BURNED

TIES

12"

12"

18"

TIES

CANES ON GROUND
GREW DURING LAST
SUMMER

AFTER OLD CANES
HAVE BEEN BURNED,
TIE NEW CANES ON
GROUND TO WIRES
AS ABOVE

PRUNING SYSTEM FOR

BOYSENBERRY - YOUNGBERRY - LOGANBERRY
BLACKBERRY - DEWBERRY - VICTORBERRY
AND OTHERS .

Berries

BOYSENBERRY | YOUNGBERRY | LOGANBERRY
BLACKBERRY | DEWBERRY | VICTORBERRY

There are many varieties of the bramble fruits that will respond to one system of pruning because of their similar habit of producing fruit. Namely, those that produce their fruit on one year old canes.

None of the listed types will require pruning the first year they are planted. Pruning will begin the second winter after planting. However, with the development of varieties that bloom and fruit on first year growth, knowing what variety you are growing is important.

If you are growing an older variety that only fruits on year old growth, then the first summer, the plants may be allowed to sprawl on the ground at will, because there will be no fruit on this first summer's growth, and the sprawling canes will provide some measure of insulation or protection of the soil around the roots.

During the first winter, a trellis or frame must be built on which to place the now fully matured canes.

Any one of several types of frame may be used, but perhaps the easiest to build will be a simple, threewire fence-type of frame. The first wire should be about one and a half feet above the ground, next wire one foot above the first, and the top wire one foot above the second. The wires should be lined up directly over the row, or series of hills where the vines have been planted. Be sure that the end posts are firmly set and braced as they must support considerable weight each summer. The wire may be tightened during the winter after the season's cutting back has been done and the wires are free of weight.

Once the wires are stretched, the berry canes which grew the previous summer and now are sprawling on the ground should be tied up on the wires. In doing this, take care to spread the canes evenly on the wires so that it will be easy to pick the berries. Wherever possible it is advisable to twine the cane once around the wire before tying with plastic tie tape. Never use wire for tying.

The pruning, which will be necessary every winter on established berry vines, is simple in its routine.

First, go down the row cutting out all of the old canes which are tied on the wires. A pair of long handled shears may be used so that the old canes may be cut off at the ground level without too much bending down. After the old canes have been cut off they should be cleared away and disposed of.

The next procedure is to tie up the new crop of canes that sprawl on the ground and which grew during the past summer.

In tying up these canes it will be easier to start with those which are shorter, training these in a more vertical position, twining the cane once around each wire as you reach it. It will be necessary to use string only near the tip of the cane, just to hold it in position. Be careful not to bend a cane too sharply, as they are apt to break.

After the short canes are tied up the longer ones may be trained out fanwise, in such spacing that the finished job will show an even distribution of canes on the wires. The more evenly the canes are spread on the wires, the better the sunlight penetration to the ripening fruit, which contributes to the sweetness of the berries.

The main thing to remember in the pruning of these types of berry fruits is that fruit is borne on canes which have grown through one summer. After this growth has produced one crop of fruit it will not set another satisfactory crop, even if it were left on the plant. When the old canes are cut out, cut them off at ground level. The new shoots will appear as suckers from below ground. Allow all of them to grow, except those that appear as suckers, away from the main hill or row.

If you are growing a newer variety which blooms and fruits on the same years growth, you will get two crops per year. An early crop on the year old canes, and a later crop from the new canes. Except for not removing the first year canes after fruiting, the care is the same.

This type of berry plant is a heavy feeder and likes a moist condition for its roots. Compost will be best for fertilizing during the winter, and feed regularly during the growing season.

Cherry

The most important part of pruning a Cherry tree is in the training that the tree receives during its first four or five years after setting out. If the training has been properly done during this period, the mature tree will require very little attention from then on in the way of pruning.

This primary care is more important with the sweet varieties of Cherries, than with the sour types, because all of the Sweet Cherries are naturally very tall growers, and are inclined to develop very weak crotches when allowed to retain all of their top growth. This pruning method is to promote a strong framework tree, rather than for increased fruit production. Pruning should be done during winter months.

When the Cherry tree is first planted, it is frequently a straight whip with no lateral branches. At the time of planting, this whip should be cut off, or headed, at about twenty-five inches above ground. This takes care of its first pruning! As the new growth starts out, select three shoots in the top eighteen inches of growth, about six inches apart up and down the stem, as shown in the chapter devoted to the "Training of Young Trees." Keep all other lateral shoots rubbed off, allowing all of the strength to go into these three framework branches.

Next year, cut back these three framework branches to about one-third to one-half their season's growth length, and during the following summer, select two well spaced shoots to develop on each of the three framework branches, rubbing off any other laterals as they appear.

The next season, repeat the directions of the last paragraph selecting two shoots on each of the previous year's growth, and continue as above until the tree is four or five years old. From this point on, the tree will practically take care of itself, with the exception of removing any branches which are interfering with other limbs, always remove the branch which is least desirable to the general shape of the tree.

Sour Cherries will only require the training period for three years, and thereafter it will be necessary to thin out the top, or fruiting wood, every winter, because of the nature of the bearing wood to grow into a tangle of small branches. In doing this thinning, cut out enough of the twig growth to eliminate a tangled appearance, and so that the branches are evenly spaced throughout the top.

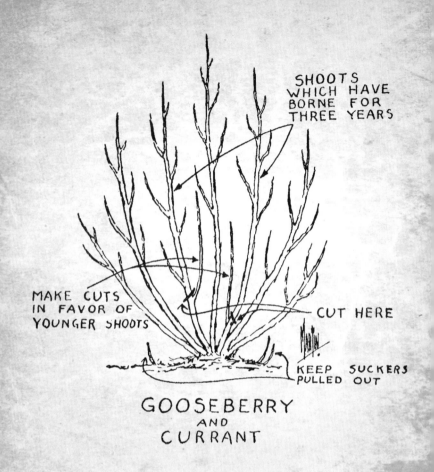

SHOOTS
WHICH HAVE
BORNE FOR
THREE YEARS

MAKE CUTS
IN FAVOR OF
YOUNGER SHOOTS

CUT HERE

KEEP SUCKERS
PULLED OUT

GOOSEBERRY
AND
CURRANT

Currant

The most satisfactory way to grow Currants for fruit production is by the bush method, where you have an opportunity to renew the fruiting wood. This system is extremely simple and is perfectly natural for the plant.

The main thing to remember in the pruning of Currants is that a cane that develops from the base of the plant will produce a good crop of fruit for three seasons, and from then on the quality and amount of fruit produced on this same cane will decrease. To take advantage of this natural characteristic of the plant, one should cut out any canes after they have produced three successive crops of fruit. In making these cuts, follow the cane to its base and cut the whole growth out, leaving a short stub above the ground about four inches long.

If there is a new, strong growth coming up near the base of the cane to be cut out, make your cut just above this shoot, so that it will receive all the strength that formerly went into the old wood.

The best time of year to do this pruning will be the winter months, although in the milder climates, summer pruning may be done where there is not the danger of the plant's suffering from "winter kill." For general practice, however, the dormant season or winter pruning is recommended.

A mature Currant plant will carry twelve good strong canes with their branches, and it is advisable to limit the plants to this amount of top growth. This limiting may be done by cutting back any greater number of canes as they start their spring and early summer growth, always leaving the strongest new canes.

In the event that the canes of Currants become infested with borers, which will be reflected by a generally unhealthy appearance of the entire cane, cut that cane out completely and put it in a plastic bag for disposal to prevent the infestation from spreading to the remainder of the plant or neighboring bushes.

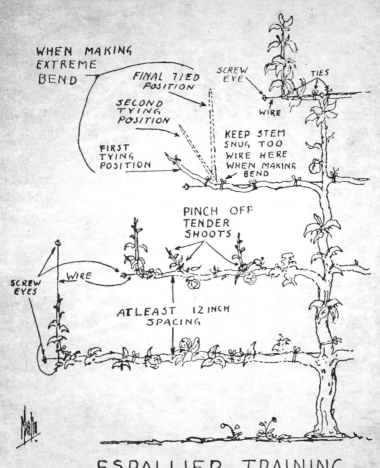

WHEN MAKING
EXTREME
BEND

FINAL TIED
POSITION

SECOND
TYING
POSITION

FIRST
TYING
POSITION

SCREW
EYE

TIES

WIRE

KEEP STEM
SNUG TOO
WIRE HERE
WHEN MAKING
BEND

PINCH OFF
TENDER
SHOOTS

SCREW
EYES

WIRE

ATLEAST 12 INCH
SPACING

ESPALLIER TRAINING

Espalier Training

This method of training fruit trees and many types of ornamental shrubs, has long been practiced in various parts of the world, and is now becoming more and more popular in this country. Where this work is done well, it is very interesting, and adds to the artistic arrangement of a landscape planting.

This article will deal only with the fundamental practice of Espalier work, rather than confine the instructions to the development of any one form or shape of frame. The shape to which the plant is to be trained will vary according to the location in which it is to be used.

Because the training of any Espalier may spread over several years, it might be better to sketch a design to be followed, suitable to the location, and then keep this sketch for reference.

The variety of plant to be used should be decided between yourself and your nursery professional, so as to obtain the best results. The selection of the individual plant is very important. Choose one that already has branches located in such distribution along the stem as to be easily trained to the basic framework of the Espalier. Where deciduous plants are to be used, the work should be started during the dormant season, because with most plants, the branches are less brittle during this time of year.

Fast growing plants are not the best to use, because they are too difficult to confine to the limits of an Espaliered design. Make your selection from a variety of plants which produce stocky branches with abundant leaves, flowers or fruit.

Care should be taken also in the selection of the variety. Choose a type of plant that will produce flowers or fruit on the same branches indefinitely. The Apple tree is an excellent example, because once its fruit spurs are developed on the branches they will produce blossoms and fruit on the same wood year after year.

The primary training of any Espaliered plant is of the utmost importance because once a branch is bent to a desired position and tied firmly there for a period of at least one year, it will remain in that position throughout the life of the plant.

In the initial training, a great deal of care should be exercised in doing the bending and tying. Where it is necessary to make a complete right-angle bend, the branch will not stand such a radical change in direction all at once without danger of breaking. To avoid this possible destruction, it will be necessary to bend the branch not more than one quarter of the complete bend, and leave it tied in this position for a period of two weeks to a month; then bend and tie a little more and leave for another period of two weeks to a month; keeping this up until the complete bend has been accomplished. Before starting any bends, be sure that the branch is tied firmly immediately below the bend, as this will help in maintaining a more symmetrical Espalier.

In order to maintain an Espalier, it will be necessary to do some minor pruning through the growing period by removing any new growth that appears in undesirable locations and favoring growth which may be used for further training or fruit production.

Summer pruning is necessary to keep the plant confined to its framework, and when this work is done, do not trim out the entire young shoot, instead pinch off the tender tip of the shoot which will stop its length growth and develop the closely set buds and leaves which are at the base of any new twig growth.

When an Espalier is first started, it is easy to develop the main framework branches too close together. Remember that the plant is going to be there for many years, and that as it grows, the growth is going to get coarser. So if the framework branches are trained about 12 inches apart, the finished effect will always be about right.

Espaliered plants may be very beautiful. However, when they do not receive the proper attention, they present an unkempt condition. If you are willing to give an Espaliered plant a few minutes of attention every month regularly, you will have some very beautiful plants trained in this system.

In the case of fruits such as Pears and Plums, which produce fruit on the same spurs year after year, do not prune the spurs out, as they never attain great length and may always be counted upon for flowers and fruit, as well as leaves.

It will be necessary to check up on your tying several times during the growing season because as a branch expands the tie becomes tighter, and if not renewed from time to time it may completely choke off the circulation of sap in the branch. The best material to use for tying is a plastic tie tape. Never use wire as this not only bruises the bark of a branch but is more difficult to undo for retying.

Feijoa or Pineapple Guava

Like many of the subtropical plants, this one bears its fruit on current season, or new wood. Therefore one must be very careful not to do any heading back when pruning.

The best time of year to do any necessary pruning is just after the fruit has all fallen from the tree. About all that will be needed is a thinning out of interfering branches or to remove any limbs which might be rubbing one another.

The natural growing habit of a Feijoa is that of a large semi-spreading shrub, and it is a mistake to attempt to force the plant into any other form by the practice of external hedging, because in so doing, the fruiting possibilities will be largely destroyed.

When the fruit of the Feijoa is ripe it will fall to the ground, where it should be harvested. Never attempt to pick the fruit from the tree.

As the plant grows it will become necessary to re-shape its growth from time to time, by encouraging the growth of new branches in the center of the head, because a heavy crop will often distort the branches. Lowering branches also must be pruned off as they drop too low.

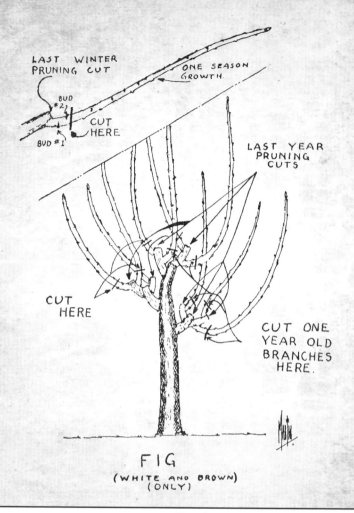

LAST WINTER
PRUNING CUT

ONE SEASON
GROWTH.

BUD
#2

CUT
HERE

BUD #1

LAST YEAR
PRUNING
CUTS

CUT
HERE

CUT ONE
YEAR OLD
BRANCHES
HERE.

FIG
(WHITE AND BROWN)
(ONLY)

WHITE | BROWN | BLACK

Figs may be divided into two classes regarding their pruning. In the first group would be the white and brown figs, which require heavy annual pruning, and the second group would be the black figs, which with their different habit of fruit production, require other treatment.

SYSTEM NUMBER ONE

White and Brown Figs (vs. Kadota, Thompson, Brown Turkey, White Pacific, Adriatic, etc.)

These varieties produce their best fruit on current season's wood, or that is, they bear fruit this year on branches which are produced and growing this year.

Because of this, the branches which were produced during the past summer should be cut back heavily during the dormant period or winter months.

In this pruning system, the branches should be cut back to two bud spurs. Or, cut the branch off about one half inch above the second bud or leaf scar from the base of the branch.

If the tree is in normal health and vigor, each of the two buds will put out growth in the spring, which in turn will produce figs during the summer, and in the following dormant period these branches must be cut back as described above. This system of heavy pruning is needed every year.

In the case of a newly planted tree, it will be advisable to start it out with a fairly low head, or crotch. The best type tree to plant should be a single "whip," with possibly a few lateral branches. When the tree is planted, it should be cut off at a height of 20 to 24 inches above the ground. Then do not allow more than three new branches to grow during the first season. Select three branches that are evenly spaced around the trunk. (See instructions on "Training of Young Trees.")

The better figs will be produced on the fast growing branches which will result from this heavy cutting back. If the tree is allowed to go untrimmed, the fruit will be of inferior size and quality. A normal young tree will frequently put out many new branches which will grow from six to eight feet during a summer and produce a fig at practically every leaf base or axis.

SYSTEM NUMBER TWO

Black Figs (vs. Mission, San Pedro, etc.)

This type of fig produces fruit on wood that is one year old and older, so an entirely different system of pruning must be followed in order to get fruit production.

The black fig, when planted, should be headed, or cut back to about two feet from the ground in order to induce a rapid first year's "framework" growth. Three branches will be enough for the tree to support during the first summer. Don't expect any figs the first year.

If your black fig tree is to be used as a combination shade tree and fruit producer, it may be headed higher to allow for its spreading branches higher off the ground, and in such a case, cut the top off at about four feet from the ground.

After the tree has made its first summer's growth, all the winter pruning will be to thin out any interfering or rubbing branches, and see to it that the top is kept evenly spaced.

Because all figs are inclined to "bleed" profusely when cut while the sap is active, the pruning should take place during the dormant period only, in the winter months while no leaves are on the branches.

Any kind of grass, such as lawn, growing over the feeder roots of figs, as well as other fruit trees, will have a tendency to deprive the fruit of its full amount of sugar, so maintain a cultivated area beneath the tree that is slightly larger than the total diameter of the top spread.

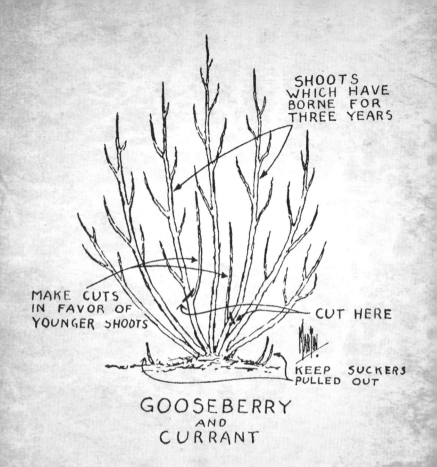

SHOOTS
WHICH HAVE
BORNE FOR
THREE YEARS

MAKE CUTS
IN FAVOR OF
YOUNGER SHOOTS

CUT HERE

KEEP SUCKERS
PULLED OUT

GOOSEBERRY
AND
CURRANT

Gooseberry

This variety of fruit is one which takes care of itself to a certain extent, but the quality of fruit may be greatly improved if the bushes are pruned every winter, after the plants are four years old. The reason for this wait being that a branch will bear good fruit for three years, after attaining one full year's growth, but after it has borne for three seasons the quality and size of the berries will decrease, therefore the necessity of pruning.

Because Gooseberries will produce to some extent on the same branches year after year without pruning, it is very easy to understand why this plant is sometimes so neglected.

When a branch starts its growth from the base of the plant, it requires one full season of growing before it is sufficiently mature to produce fruit.

The pruning procedure is to allow this cane to stay on the bush during three fruiting periods and then cut it out to make way for new bearing wood. When taking out the branch, make the cut down to the base of the plant, leaving a stub from six to seven inches in length upon which new shoots will sprout. The pruning should be done during the winter months.

The following spring, there may be many new shoots which will start out from the stub, but allow only about three of the strongest to grow. Pull the others off while they are still soft.

Although it may be a temptation to leave all of the fruit producing branches, a well established plant will produce many pounds of fruit and it is better to have this poundage in large sized fruit rather than a great abundance of undersized berries. This system of pruning will insure the right type of wood on the bush that will produce the largest berries possible.

Grapefruit or Pomelo

Like many of the citrus trees, there is little to be done to a Grapefruit tree as far as pruning is concerned. Under average conditions, it will not be necessary to prune the tree at all until it is at least five years old, because their growth is uniform in its habits, and the tree will practically shape itself.

The only pruning that might be necessary on a young Grapefruit tree is to remove any rubbing or crossing branches, and any branches touching the ground. Where branches of citrus trees have an opportunity to rub against one another causing a breaking of the bark, it makes it very easy for disease to start from such a wound. In removing a rubbing or crossing branch, cut out the one which contributes the least to the general shape of the tree. Branches touching the ground allow vermin access to the tree and should be cut back.

Because of the extremely dense growth habit of the Grapefruit, as time goes on, there will always be a certain amount of dead twigs on the inside of the tree. These should be cut off, so that the die-back will not travel into the living branches. This cutting out of the dead twigs should be done twice a year, six months apart. In this way, the twig will be cut off before it has died completely to the main branch, which will allow the cut to heal better.

As the Grapefruit develops size, there will be less and less foliage on the inside of the tree so it will be easier to see what pruning will be needed by standing on the inside of the tree. There will usually be room enough in between the branches to move one's arms around sufficiently to do the necessary thinning out. By standing on the ground with your head and body inside the head of the tree, one may notice where the branches are growing denser in some spots than in others. These overly thick collections of twig growth should be thinned out to allow a slight penetration of sunlight. This work requires the thinning out of only small twigs, because large holes should not be opened up suddenly by heavier pruning.

This pruning may be done at any time of the year, because by following this system, it will probably not be necessary to cut out any actual fruit-bearing wood. However, pruning during the winter, or cool weather, would be better for the tree.

Do not allow any branches to hang down to within one foot of the ground, as this makes it more possible for various fungus diseases to infect any low hanging fruit which might be borne on them.

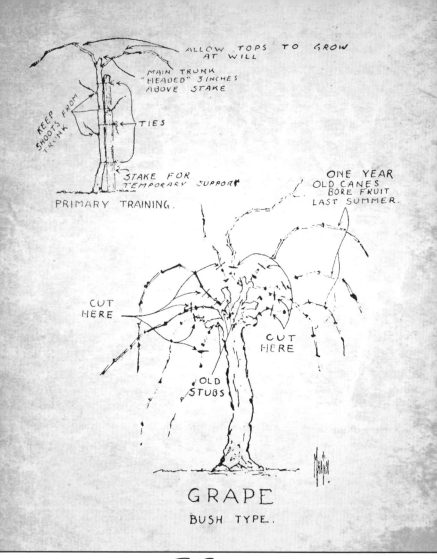

ALLOW TOPS TO GROW AT WILL

MAIN TRUNK "HEADED" 3 INCHES ABOVE STAKE

KEEP SHOOTS FROM TRUNK

TIES

STAKE FOR TEMPORARY SUPPORT

PRIMARY TRAINING.

ONE YEAR OLD CANES BORE FRUIT LAST SUMMER.

CUT HERE

CUT HERE

OLD STUBS

GRAPE
BUSH TYPE.

Grape

There are two general types of Grapes, namely bush and vine. Their respective systems of pruning will be taken up separately. Also because either one may be grown for fruit production alone, or as an arbor plant, the pruning system for each type will be taken up individually.

BUSH TYPE GRAPES

(Such as Muscat, Malaga, Thompson Seedless, Tokay, etc.)
Grown for fruit production only.

The first year that the grape is planted should be devoted to training only. Place a vertical stake by the plant so that there is two feet of stake above ground and allow only one cane to grow by selecting the strongest and cutting off all other lateral or side shoots which may start. This will force all of the season's growth into the one cane which may be tied at intervals to the stake to keep the stem straight. When the one cane reaches the top of the stake, tie it firmly and allow it to sprawl around at will for the rest of the growing period.

During the winter, the main cane should be cut off, about two inches above the top of the stake. In the spring when the new growth starts, allow only the two top buds, or joints, to send out shoots. Cut off smooth with the side of the branch any shoots which appear on what may now be called the trunk, or stem.

Through the summer growing season, allow these two shoots, or canes, to make whatever growth they will without further training or pruning. There may or may not be some grapes set on this growth. If they do set, the plant will be strong enough to ripen them so they may be left.

Now will begin the regular annual system which must be followed every winter. The preceding instructions cover the initial training period only.

During the winter season while the grape is dormant is the time that the pruning should be done. All canes that grew the past summer must be cut back to just above the second bud or joint from the base of the one year old canes. There will always be a group of latent buds right at the base of the cane, which will only be forced in case the other buds are damaged in some way. Count out from the base of the cane two buds or joints and cut the cane off about one half inch beyond the second bud.

If the plant is strong, both of these buds will start growing in the spring, and if they do, leave them. Bunches of grapes will appear on this new growth which has started from the short stubs that were left.

Be sure to do the pruning as soon as possible in the fall after the leaves have all dropped because at this time there is no sap activity and the canes will not bleed as a result of being cut.

As soon as the trunk is large enough to support itself, remove the stake and do not rely on further support or tying.

BUSH TYPE GRAPES FOR ARBORS

There are no set rules which must be followed as to any particular type of trellis or arbor for grape training. Grapes will adapt themselves to almost any type of screen or arbor, providing they get plenty of sun for ripening their fruit.

When growing grapes for arbors, the initial training is of all-importance and should be attended to at least once every two weeks through the growing period. A grape arbor will produce its best fruit on top, so it is inadvisable to try to maintain any fruit production on the sides. For this reason, force all the growth into one main cane which is to be trained vertically up the side of the arbor. This main cane may be either twined around the upright post or tied to it. Discourage any lateral growth along this main stem by rubbing off any side buds as they appear.

As soon as the vine has reached the top of the arbor, the fruit producing wood may be developed. The canes should either be twined around the supporting wire or trellis in fanwise or parallel form, keeping any parallel canes about 12 or 15 inches apart. This growth will be the permanent framework from which the fruit will be produced every year for an indefinite period, so be very careful and exacting with the training of the permanent canes. Do not try to get fruit production from any cane until it has made its full growth as foundation wood. It may take several seasons to get full coverage from the foundation wood. However, as any foundation cane reaches its full development, the pruning for fruit production may begin the following winter.

Once the canes are established, they will begin to put out fruit producing wood the following year. These permanent canes will produce fruit year after year indefinitely when properly pruned.

The pruning procedure to follow is very simple. During the winter months, as soon as the leaves have dried and fallen, cut back all of the canes which grew during the past summer, including those which produced fruit. Cut them back to within two buds or joints above their base. New fruit bearing canes will grow from one or both of the buds which were left.

As time goes on the framework branches will become very heavy, with increasing size, but this condition will not affect the fruiting possibilities of the vine. As long as the annual wood is renewed systematically each year, the vine will produce good sized bunches indefinitely.

VINING TYPE GRAPES
(Such as Eastern Concord, etc.)

This type of grape includes those more immediately descended from the wild grapes of the woods, and they are all natural climbers, therefore requiring a specific treatment in order to obtain the best production from them.

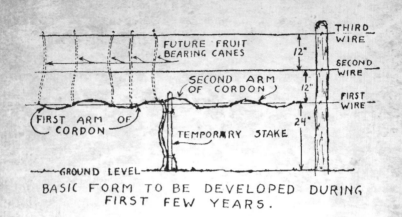

THIRD WIRE

SECOND WIRE

FIRST WIRE

FUTURE FRUIT BEARING CANES   12"

SECOND ARM OF CORDON   12"

FIRST ARM OF CORDON   24"

TEMPORARY STAKE

GROUND LEVEL

BASIC FORM TO BE DEVELOPED DURING FIRST FEW YEARS.

VINING TYPE GRAPES

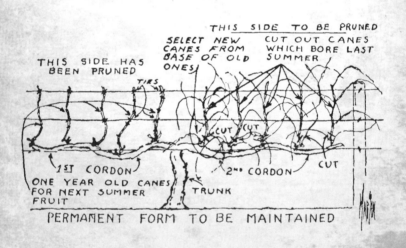

THIS SIDE TO BE PRUNED

SELECT NEW CANES FROM BASE OF OLD ONES

CUT OUT CANES WHICH BORE LAST SUMMER

THIS SIDE HAS BEEN PRUNED

TIES

CUT   CUT

1ST CORDON

2ND CORDON

CUT

ONE YEAR OLD CANES FOR NEXT SUMMER FRUIT

TRUNK

PERMANENT FORM TO BE MAINTAINED

There have been many systems of training developed for these grapes, some of them quite complicated. The simplest form of training, and one which will assure the grower of a good yield with the least amount of work, is the one referred to as the "two arm Cordon" system, which includes the construction of a three wire "fence" type of trellis.

The construction of this type of trellis should be done with an eye to the future; that is, do not use light materials for the end posts and their bracing. The posts and wires must support a great deal of weight as years go by, so sturdy construction is required.

Where a three wire trellis is used, which by the way will give the most satisfactory support for the vines, the lower wire should be stretched tight, two feet from the ground. The second wire one foot above the lower, and the third, or top wire, one foot above the second.

The young vines should be planted 10 feet apart, directly under the wires, and then the training may commence as the vines grow. If the following training is done carefully for the first few years it will greatly simplify the pruning in future years. Each vine can be trained into an almost exact duplicate of all the others.

As the young vine grows, it may be held in place with a light vertical stake until it gets up to about the height of the first wire, then this temporary stake may be removed and the first arm of the cordon started on its training. When the growth starts in the spring, select one good strong shoot which has forced out from the base of last year's growth.

Cut off all other shoots, forcing all of the growth into one sturdy cane. Do not even allow any lateral or side shoots to grow from the one cane until the first or lowest wire is reached. Then if a shoot develops at this level it may be used for training the second arm of the cordon.

Just as soon as the young shoot is long enough to twine around the first wire, start the training by twining it around the wire. This initial training may go on for two or three years, depending upon the growth that the plant makes. Keep up the training of this first cane until the tip has reached five feet out on the wire, and then pinch off the tip or terminal bud, to stop its horizontal growth.

In the meantime, the training may be started on the arm in the opposite direction, by allowing as previously mentioned, a bud to grow, which has started at about the point where the main trunk meets the lower wire. Train this cane, as with the other one, until it has reached a point five feet from the main stem in the opposite direction.

Now there should be the main stem or trunk and the two arms of the cordon stretching in opposite directions, supported by the lower wire, forming a T with a broad top bar.

This "two armed cordon" is the permanent framework from which the fruit bearing canes will develop year after year. Where pruning is done properly, each joint or bud on these cordons produces fruit bearing canes each year as long as the vine survives.

This type of grape produces fruit from the first three to five joints, or buds, on canes which have grown during the previous summer. This same cane will not produce fruit again.

Allow the canes which spring out on each arm to grow as they wish during the summer, without any tying. During the winter dormant period, select about five of the strongest, one year old canes, on each arm, and tie them vertically to the two wires above. For this purpose use either twine or vinyl tie tape. Never use copper wire. Cut the tied canes about three inches above the top wire.

All other canes which have grown from the arm should now be cut back, leaving two buds above their base.

Each cane which has been tied in this manner should produce about three bunches of good-sized grapes, and with 10 canes tied, you'll get about 30 bunches of grapes for each vine.

The next winter remove the canes which are tied up, cutting them off just above one good strong shoot which has grown from its base. After the last year's fruit canes have been removed, tie up the new strong canes, as before, selecting five from each arm, and continue this treatment year after year.

Where treated right, the Concords and similar varieties, in California, have out-produced their parent vineyards in the Eastern states, as well as producing a higher quality grape.

VINE TYPE GRAPES FOR ARBORS
Same training as for "Bush Type Grapes For Arbors."

Strawberry Guava

RED OR YELLOW

Like many of the subtropical fruits, the red or yellow Guavas require little in the way of pruning because of their fruiting habits. The fruit is borne on new wood.

The growth of these plants is very shrubby by nature, and because of this the bushes will require very little shaping. The only pruning necessary, therefore, is that which the location of the plant might govern. Where Guavas have been used as ornamental plants it may become necessary to trim out any branches which are growing out of bounds, too tall, or too spreading.

The best time of year to do this pruning is in the winter months, while the plants are experiencing little or no growth.

In the case of an old hedge of guavas that has grown too tall and is rather unsightly due to their open habit of growth, the plants may be cut back and the hedge started all over again. In cutting of this sort, cut off all growth about two feet from the ground during the late winter months. This severe treatment may spoil one season's fruit production but the plants will throw out masses of new shoots from the old stems which will make a new low hedge of attractive appearance.

Pruning will not increase fruit production of the Guavas, therefore this work is a matter of individual plant shape.

Lemon

There are many systems for the pruning of Lemon trees, all of which have been worked out to apply to orchard conditions for various localities in which the fruit is grown, and they are proving successful wherever they are used consistently.

The system most easily adapted to the amateur grower of Lemons, where there are from one to three trees in a yard, is as follows and is a system which takes advantage of the natural growing habit of the tree and will require the least amount of attention.

Pruning may be done on a Lemon where one uses the following system, at any time of the year when it becomes necessary, because lemons are flowering and fruiting constantly.

Under average circumstances, a lemon tree will require no pruning for the first four years after it has been planted, except to trim out any branch which rubs against another, and to rub off any sucker shoots which might appear on the trunk or stem. In removing these shoots, it is better to rub them off or pull them, rather than cut them, because cutting encourages regrowth of more shoots.

The natural habit of a Lemon tree after it is well established, is to send out long upright fast growing shoots from the center of the head, which in time become heavy at the tip with foliage and then begins to gradually bend down. This natural habit may be used to develop a very productive tree, and one which will have very large fruit, all during the year.

Like many citrus trees it is not advisable to allow any branches within about two feet from the ground, because of the danger of fungus infection of fruit, and access of insects to the tree. As the lower branches are carried lower each year with the weight of fruit and foliage, they may be cut off and that energy forced into the development of other branches. Cut these off well back into the head of the tree where they leave a main limb. Make a smooth cut outside the collar.

The long spindling upright shoots which appear during the summer months in the center of the tree, will in time, make good fruiting wood so they should be left, except where too many spring out in one place. In this case, select one of the strongest and cut out the others. As these tall shoots reach the top of the tree they will begin to develop lateral twigs and heavy foliage, which will cause them to bend down in an arching habit. As they come down, remove any branches which might get in their way. As this wood matures it will begin to set fruit, and the Lemons nearest the ends of these branches are usually the finest quality.

This system of growing may be carried on indefinitely, constantly renewing the fruit bearing wood. The tree may not be the most symmetrical in shape, but it will produce an abundance of high quality Lemons.

As the limbs get too close to the ground (two feet), cut the branch out and develop new ones from the inside of the tree's head. From the time that one of these upright branches starts its growth to the time when it is necessary to be removed because it has grown too close to the ground, will be anywhere from five to 10 years.

The dwarf bush Lemon will require practically no pruning, except to cut out any interfering branches, and as the limbs bend down to the ground, to cut them off well back inside the plant which will force new growth in more desirable locations.

Lime

There are many species of Lime grown commercially, as well as in the backyard garden, but they all have the same requirements as far as pruning is concerned. As trees go, the Lime will shape itself into a very symmetrical top.

Any sucker growth that appears on the stem should be rubbed off as it appears. Where these shoots are allowed to grow, they will take most of the vitality which should go into the top.

Watch out for any rubbing or crossing branches that may have grown in the top. Remove the one which contributes the least to the general good shape of the tree. The heaviest cutting should be done during the winter months, whenever necessary.

Loquat

There are few fruit trees that require less trimming than the Loquat. In fact, this variety could grow very successfully with no pruning at all.

Loquat trees should be headed quite low when they are first set out, because as the tree develops there is a constant subdividing of terminal growth, causing the general shape of the tree to be an inverted pyramid.

The only pruning to be done is to cut out any dead branches and to pull off any sucker growth that appears below the head or from the roots.

As this fruit is a member of the Apple family, it is subject to "Fire Blight," a bacterial disease which attacks all in this family. The disease may be recognized by the sudden dying of twig tips and leaves, almost as though the leaves had been burned by fire. When this occurs, cut out the infected branch at least a foot beyond any show of infection. The disease travels in the sap, so it may be further down the twig than the leaves show. Cut far enough to be safe, and sterilize shears between cuts.

Loquat pruning should be done in early fall so that the tree may fully recover before the fruit buds start to develop.

Nectarine

The pruning of this fruit is very similar to that of its close family member, the Peach, except that it will not be necessary to prune quite so heavily. The fruit is borne on one year old branches, not on spurs, so the fruiting wood must be renewed every season.

For training young Nectarine trees, see the chapter on "Training Young Trees."

The Nectarine, like the Peach, will set its best fruit in the center one-third section of one year old branches. Keep this in mind as the tree is shaped and pruned. Pruning must be done during the dormant period in winter.

When the pruning actually begins the procedure is as follows:

First, remove any dead or interfering wood from the tree top, along with any branches which bore fruit last year. All suckers on the stem should be removed as they appear during the summer.

Second, select the strongest branches with the most amount of lateral twig growth for the fruit producing wood. This twig growth is the fruiting wood for the coming season. Thin out any branches in such a way as to leave an evenly spaced branch-work in the top.

Third, thin out the fruiting twigs so that they are spaced about eight inches to one foot apart all over the tree.

Fourth, clip back all of the remaining fruiting twigs (one year old) to one-third their length. This procedure will leave enough fruit buds for the tree to care for. Do not do any hand thinning of fruit until after the normal June drop has occurred. The tree will carry and mature all fruit left after this natural thinning process.

Avoid propping the limbs unless absolutely necessary. In the event the use of props is needed, however, remove them just as soon as the fruit is off the tree because their continued use will cause a weakening of the branch structure.

For illustration governing the pruning of Nectarine, see the one covering pruning of Peaches. The fundamentals are the same.

Orange

Citrus fruits in general require very little in the way of pruning and the Orange, regardless of whether it is Navel, Valencia, or other varieties, is no exception. These fruits have a habit of growth which virtually trains themselves for the first four to seven years, leaving very little for the owner to attend except to irrigate and fertilize properly.

As with all citrus trees, the Orange develops a head with very close set leaves, excluding practically all sunlight from the inside of the tree. This condition causes minor die-back of small twigs on the inside of the tree.

Watch out for any crossing or interfering branches which may be rubbing against each other. Cut out the interfering branch which contributes the least to the general good shape of the tree.

As the Orange tree grows older, the outer branches will bend lower toward the ground. As they droop to less than two feet from the ground, the ends should be removed to prevent fungus disease from spreading from the soil to the fruit on the lower branches. This pruning should be done as soon as the fruit has been picked from these lowering branches.

Remove any shoots or suckers that may appear on the trunk of the tree. If these are removed when they are only an inch or two in length they may be rubbed off by a downward movement of the hand against the tree trunk.

Orange branches are sufficiently tough to withstand a considerable load of fruit without breaking, and even though an overload of fruit may distort the position of a branch, do not put a prop under a heavily laden limb to help support the fruit because this action will cause a very rapid weakening of the limb itself. Props are to be avoided except as a very last resort.

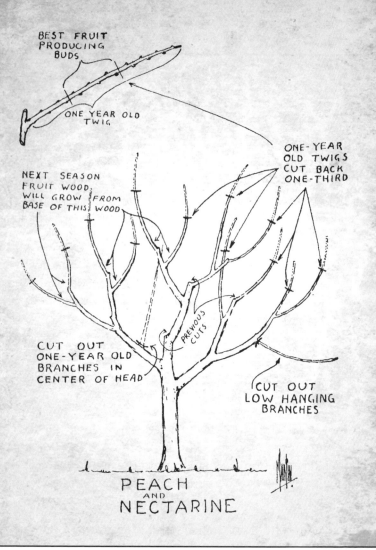

BEST FRUIT
PRODUCING
BUDS

ONE YEAR OLD
TWIG

ONE-YEAR
OLD TWIGS
CUT BACK
ONE-THIRD

NEXT SEASON
FRUIT WOOD,
WILL GROW FROM
BASE OF THIS WOOD

PREVIOUS
CUTS

CUT OUT
ONE-YEAR OLD
BRANCHES IN
CENTER OF HEAD

CUT OUT
LOW HANGING
BRANCHES

PEACH
AND
NECTARINE

Peach

There are few fruit trees that benefit from heavy pruning as
does the Peach. The size and quality of the fruit is governed by
whether or not the tree is properly pruned. This pruning is to
be done during the winter dormant period.

Peaches require a heavier removal of old wood than any other fruit tree. Frequently it will be necessary to prune out as much as seventy to seventy-five percent of the previous season's growth.

The Peach bears its fruit quite differently than any other type of tree, and this characteristic must be thoroughly understood. The fruit will appear on the twigs and branches which grew during the past summer. Although there will be blossoms the entire length of these twigs, the only flowers that should be allowed to set the fruit are those in the central one-third section of these twigs. Therefore, after the tree has been properly shaped by thinning, head back all of these twigs one-third of their length. Keep this in mind while doing the shaping.

The procedure to follow for the pruning of Peaches, is as follows:

First, cut out any dead branches which are on the tree. The older the tree the more of these there will be.

Second, cut out the least desirable of any crossing or rubbing branches. The branch that remains should be located as to contribute to the general good form of the tree. Also, cut out any branches that bore fruit last summer. These will not bear fruit again, so remove them.

Third, the shape to be desired for the tree is that of a funnel, with the branches forming the sloping sides and the center top left open for complete penetration of sunlight. This open center will permit better ripening of the fruit.

Fourth, begin to thin out the branches all through the tree, in such a way as to give an even distribution of branch growth throughout the entire tree. Always favor new branch growth. Do not hesitate to head back tall growth because

Peach wood is brittle and a tall tree is almost sure to shed otherwise good limbs when they are heavy with fruit. Make the cuts carefully with an eye to the location of the one year old twigs or the fruiting branches. When finished, these one year old twigs should be about one foot apart all over the top of the tree.

In the case of trees that are more than 10 years old, it may be necessary to select a new branch from the forks of the main branches to replace an old limb which has become diseased or broken.

Fifth, when the shaping has been completed, and at this point there should be better than sixty percent of the tree on the ground, it is time to head back all of the one year old twigs and allow for fruit bud development.

As noted previously, cut back all of this one year old growth, one-third of its length. This heading back throws the maximum strength into the fruit buds which have been left.

A healthy Peach tree will set a very large amount of fruit, and about the first of June, the tree will voluntarily drop a proportion of the fruit that has already partially developed. If in your opinion, there is still too much fruit for the tree to support, the fruit may be hand thinned, but wait until the voluntary June drop has taken place.

There are other systems of pruning Peach trees, some of them involving the practice of summer pruning. Summer pruning will help keep your tree smaller throughout the year, and keep more fruit lower in the tree and more easily accessible.

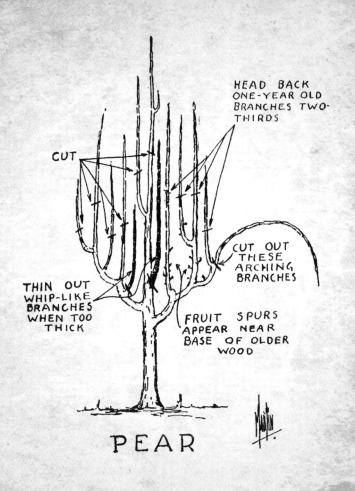

HEAD BACK ONE-YEAR OLD BRANCHES TWO-THIRDS

CUT

CUT OUT THESE ARCHING BRANCHES

THIN OUT WHIP-LIKE BRANCHES WHEN TOO THICK

FRUIT SPURS APPEAR NEAR BASE OF OLDER WOOD

PEAR

Pear

There are many varieties of Pears grown in various parts of the country. Although the habits of growth differ widely, the same system of pruning may be applied to them all. There is little similarity in growth between a dwarf variety and a Winter Nelis Pear but the same principles apply because they all produce their best fruit from fruit spurs, so the pruning to be done should favor these spurs.

Pruning is done during the winter months, while the tree is dormant.

Once again, the pruning system to be recommended is one that will apply best to the average backyard tree. There are a good many systems of pruning for orchard plantings, some of which would be practical for home use, but in order to eliminate confusion, the directions for just one method will be discussed here.

When the Pear tree is planted, the central stem should be headed, or cut off, at about thirty inches from the ground. If there are any lateral branches on the main stem, select three evenly spaced around the trunk as well as up and down the main stem and prune away the rest. See illustration on "Training Young Trees."

The first year should be devoted to training the scaffold limbs. It is more important to have a tree with a good sturdy foundation of limbs than to get minimal fruit a year early. Follow instructions of the "Training Young Trees" chapter.

The general habit of all Pear trees is to send up a great deal of tall whip-like branches from the center of the tree, especially in young trees, and the pruner must work every year to keep the head of the tree down, directing the vitality into the fruit bearing spurs, which will develop on the older wood.

The first thing to consider in the pruning of a Pear tree is the removal of any dead wood, which on young trees will be very limited.

Second, cut out any interfering or crossing branches, that is, branches which are rubbing one another. Remove the one which contributes the least to the tree's good shape.

Third, thin out any new growths of whip-like tall shoots where they have grown in an overcrowded manner.

Fourth, head back the more substantial whip growths about two-thirds of their length. This cutting will force the tree's vitality into the main body of the tree-head, causing the greatest amount of strength to go to the fruit spurs.

Fruit spurs are the short stubby growths which have been developing on the older branches. They will vary in shape and length, but most frequently have a knob-like end, which is covered with new buds. These spurs will produce fruit year after year and should never be pruned off unless they die from old age, or are killed by disease.

When the job of pruning is complete, the head of the tree should be evenly spaced allowing for an even penetration of sunlight. This is essential to the correct ripening of fruit.

Where the fruit production is kept in the lower portion of the tree head, there will be practically no need for any propping of limbs due to heavy fruit production.

There is quite a tendency in some Pear varieties to produce a great deal of new growth towards the center of the tree. Where this habit shows up, the pruner should remove these central shoots, forcing the tree into a more spreading form. Otherwise, your tree will soon become too tall for convenient picking, and the mass of central growth will cause the tree to become more of an easy prey to disease.

One of the worst diseases to attack Pear trees is a bacterial one known as "Fire Blight," which is noticeable in the sudden dying of twig ends and leaves. As this disease travels within the stems and is spread by many causes, the diseased twigs should be cut off as soon as they are noticed. When cutting out this disease, always disinfect the shears after each cut with a 10% bleach solution or 70% or 92% alcohol. Wipe off the pruners before each cut to reduce the chance of burning the cambium. Where the Blight gets into a main limb, it will be better to sacrifice the limb than to allow it to spread to the remainder of the tree. In cutting out any infected twigs, cut at least six to eight inches beyond where any infection shows up. All diseased twigs must be disposed of in a plastic garbage bag and not recycled to stop the spread of harmful bacteria. Do not compost the twigs and branches or you will reintroduce the disease.

Pecan

The most important thing to be remembered in the growing of Pecan trees is the training to proper shape during the first five years of their growth. The natural tendency of the Pecan is for the outer branches to bend lower each year, due to the weight of foliage and fruit, so the initial training should be to develop a tree with the main framework branches as erect as possible. Some lateral branches may be encouraged to provide shade for the inner portion of the head.

Due to the natural habit of growth, a Pecan tree should be headed at about six feet from the ground. By this, it is meant not to allow any lateral branches on the trunk below six feet from the ground. The top will divide of its own accord higher up so that it will not be necessary to stop the terminal growth of any upright branches, or the main central stem.

Any necessary pruning that is needed will consist of the removal of any interfering branches, and as the tree gets older, to remove the lower branches as they bend low enough to interfere with a person's walking beneath the tree. The Pecan is by nature a very tall growing tree, and as the nuts fall when ripe, there is no necessity to try to alter the natural habit of growth, which is very beautiful in its natural proportions.

Pruning should be done during the winter months, while the tree is dormant and without leaves. This tree makes a satisfactory shade tree and will require a minimum of care.

Persimmon

The initial training of any variety of Persimmon is of utmost importance. Because of the brittleness of the branches, you must develop a tree with strong and well-spaced scaffold branches. See the instructions on "Training of Young Trees," for proper training procedure.

The necessary pruning for Persimmon trees is very simple indeed. The fruit is borne on current season wood, or in other words, a branch which grows this year will produce fruit this year, also fruit is borne on the one year old branches. So heading back will deprive the tree of its production of fruit.

Therefore, the only pruning which will be needed is to keep the tree well thinned out, and an even spacing of the fruit producing branches. Cut off any branches which have bent down low enough to interfere with working around the tree. These constantly lowering branches are always being replaced by center growth on the inside of the tree.

In case a Persimmon tree becomes too tall making it difficult to pick the fruit, the tall branches may be headed back severely. New shoots will spring out below where the limb was cut, and some of these may have to be thinned out during the summer if there appears to be too many.

The time for the annual pruning is during the winter months, while the tree is without leaves and the sap is dormant.

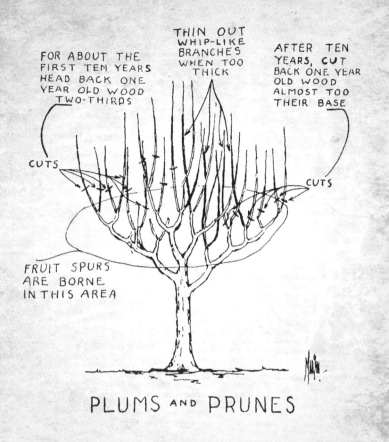

FOR ABOUT THE
FIRST TEN YEARS
HEAD BACK ONE
YEAR OLD WOOD
TWO-THIRDS

THIN OUT
WHIP-LIKE
BRANCHES
WHEN TOO
THICK

AFTER TEN
YEARS, CUT
BACK ONE YEAR
OLD WOOD
ALMOST TOO
THEIR BASE

CUTS

CUTS

FRUIT SPURS
ARE BORNE
IN THIS AREA

PLUMS AND PRUNES

Plum and Prune

These two fruits are the same with the exception that Prunes have greater sugar content and therefore will dry without removing the pit. One system of pruning will apply to both types because they all have the same fruiting habits. Prune the trees in the winter while the trees are dormant.

Plums and Prunes do their best fruit producing from fruit spurs, which may appear on any branch after it is two or more years old. Therefore the pruning system should be one which will develop these fruit spurs.

These two fruits are the same with the exception that Prunes have greater sugar content and therefore will dry without removing the pit. One system of pruning will apply to both types because they all have the same fruiting habits. Prune the trees in the winter while the trees are dormant.

Plums and Prunes do their best fruit producing from fruit spurs, which may appear on any branch after it is two or more years old. Therefore the pruning system should be one which will develop these fruit spurs.

For the training of a young Prune or Plum tree, follow the directions as specified in the chapter on "Training Young Trees."

Because of the nature of these two types of fruits, it is of utmost importance to develop a very strong and well balanced framework of branches. The general shape of the most desirable tree to be grown is that of a funnel, or inverted pyramid, with the center well filled with fruit producing limbs.

Until the tree is about 10 years old, the training program will continue by heading back the long whip-like branches about two-thirds to three-quarters of their length, where they have grown in a position to benefit the desired form for the tree. Any new branches that do not benefit the shape of the tree should be cut out entirely. Branches should be spaced not closer than one foot from each other, to allow for easy picking and light penetration.

After about the third year, the fruit spurs will begin to develop on the oldest branches, and these small gnarled, stubby growths will produce fruit year after year. Always save the branches with fruit spurs wherever possible.

When the tree is 10 years old or more, the new growth must be cut out almost entirely every winter, leaving it only where it is necessary to refill a space where an old limb has been taken out. As the outer branches gradually become lower with the weight of fruit and foliage, they should be cut out during the winter. This removal of a main limb should be balanced by leaving an equal amount of new wood on the inside of the tree to take its place.

The procedure for pruning Plum and Prune trees, 10 years old and older, would be as follows:

- First, cut out any dead wood and crossing or interfering branches.

- Second, remove any old limbs that have lowered their position to the extent of being in the way.

- Third, start removing new growth by cutting out the least desirable branches first.

When there is nothing left in new growth but those which are evenly spaced throughout the tree, head these back to about one-third to one-quarter of their length. The older the tree, the more they should be headed back.

Pomegranate

The pruning of this variety of fruit is very simple in method, but rather difficult from a standpoint of labor, due to the toughness of the wood and close habit of growing.

Natural tendency of the Pomegranate is to develop a mass of erect growing shoots or branches, which if allowed to stay will grow into a plant to which very little can be done.

For the first three or four years try to encourage as spreading a plant as possible by cutting out the shoots that spring from the lower inside of the plant. As the plant develops, allow no new shoots to grow that appear within two feet of the ground. Pull them off as they start. A single trunk bush will be much easier to care for in the future. Where young plants are set out, this type of training will be easy.

Pomegranates will produce fruit from any wood after it is one year old, but the quality and size of the fruit will be better if the top is kept well thinned out, allowing plenty of sunlight penetration.

The natural tendency for the Pomegranate is to grow into an erect arching shape, with the outer branches constantly lowering. Therefore, it will be necessary to cut out this outside growth from time to time as the necessity arises, wherever a branch is too low and in the way.

Pruning should be done during the dormant period of winter.

This fruit may be grown in two different forms, either as a tree with a single trunk, or as a bush. Because of the nature of the plant, the latter system will be the easier. The same system of pruning will apply to both methods of shaping the tree.

The manner in which the Quince bears its fruit determines the system of pruning. The best fruit buds will be found as lateral or side buds in the upper half of the one year old twigs. These same branches will produce good fruit for about three or four years so a system of thinning out the oldest branches is all that will be needed in the way of pruning.

Pruning of the Quince will not become necessary until the fourth winter of the tree's life, and then should be done every winter thereafter. Keep the top evenly spaced with upright shoots or branches, cutting out the ones which have arched over to the ground from the weight of fruit.

Do not head the branches back as this will take off all the fruiting possibilities of the plant. If the plant has become too tall, thin out the tallest branches well down into the base of the plant.

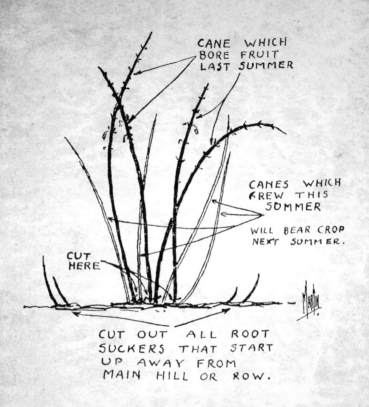

CANE WHICH BORE FRUIT LAST SUMMER

CANES WHICH GREW THIS SUMMER

WILL BEAR CROP NEXT SUMMER.

CUT HERE

CUT OUT ALL ROOT SUCKERS THAT START UP AWAY FROM MAIN HILL OR ROW.

RASPBERRY

Raspberry

The pruning instructions for raspberries, as with other of the bramble fruits, are very simple. The point to remember is that the best berries will be borne on canes which have grown one full season. In other words, canes that started from the root and grew this summer will produce berries next summer. When these canes have produced their summer crop they should be removed.

Pruning is done during the winter months while the plants are dormant.

Cut off at ground level all canes which produced fruit last season. This will leave an ample supply of young canes which have grown for one complete growing season and which will produce fruit during the coming summer.

All raspberries have a tendency to spread out over more area as a result of increased root development. As the plants grow it will become necessary to dig up some of these spreading roots in order to keep the original row or hill. These roots which have been dug up may be used for planting new areas.

Walnut

This variety requires little pruning, providing the initial training has been done properly. The young tree should be topped, or cut off, at about eight feet from the ground, and no lateral growth allowed to develop below six feet. All three framework branches should develop as specified in the "Training of Young Trees" chapter. Except that there should be about 24 inches between top and lower branches instead of 16.

The tendency for Walnut trees is for the outer branches to constantly lower each year with the weight of fruit and foliage. As these branches get low enough to interfere with cultivating, etc., they can be cut off during the winter months while the sap is inactive. Be sure that the sap is dormant by making a trial cut on a live twig, and watch it for a few minutes to see if there is excessive bleeding. If bleeding occurs make no further cuts until the sap is dormant.

To counteract the tendency of the constantly lowering outer branches, new branches should be encouraged in the center of the tree. These, as time goes on, will gradually work their way outward.

The top of the tree should be kept free of any interfering or rubbing branches as well as all dead wood. Do this at the dormant period, during the winter.

Notes

Pruning Tools

GETTING STARTED

Pruning, as with most jobs, is best done with the right tools. The right tools can save time, labor, and make the difference between a quality job and mediocre one. Since the main tools used for pruning are cutting tools, this is especially true. The sharper the tools the faster and easier they will cut, less exertion will be required, and minimal damage to remaining trunks and branches will be caused. There are a variety of cutting tools that will be used in pruning fruit trees and we will discuss the attributes of them and their specific functions.

MAKE THE INVESTMENT

A quality set of pruning shears is one of the greatest investments even a weekend gardener can make for their tool arsenal. No matter which shear you choose they should always be clean, sharp, and well adjusted before beginning your pruning job. Sharp, clean blades make for easier, cleaner cuts with less damage to the plant.

High quality shears are worth the investment. In most cases, many of the parts of these shears are replaceable, meaning a much longer life for the tool. Many high end shears have forged aluminum handles making them lightweight and reducing fatigue during long pruning jobs. In higher end shears you will also find optional features that can make a big difference in how you prune. Right and left handed shears are great as typically your dominant hand will be the stronger one making cutting easier. Some shears have a rolling handle that will reduce hand fatigue when used

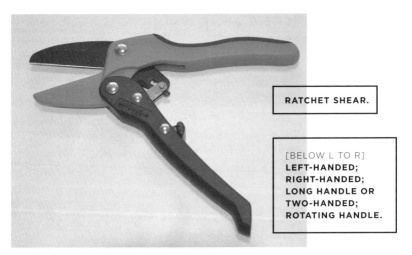

RATCHET SHEAR.

[BELOW L TO R]
**LEFT-HANDED;
RIGHT-HANDED;
LONG HANDLE OR
TWO-HANDED;
ROTATING HANDLE.**

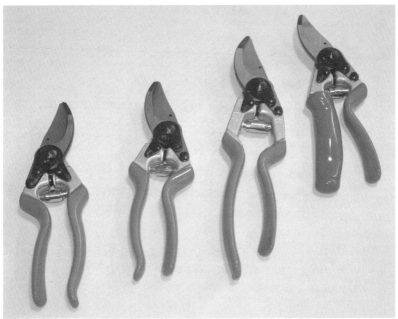

for long periods of time. Some shears have extended handles that allow easier two handed cutting extending the size of the branches that can be handled.

BYPASS PRUNERS & ANVIL PRUNERS

There are two basic types of pruning shears; bypass pruners and anvil pruners. Anvil pruners cut by having the blade cut through the branch and land on a flat anvil to complete the cut. Some gardeners do not like anvil shears as they feel the crushing action caused by the anvil damages the part of the branch that remains on the plant. Bypass shears cut with a true shearing action like a pair of scissors. If handled properly, they can cut without any damage to the remaining branch structure.

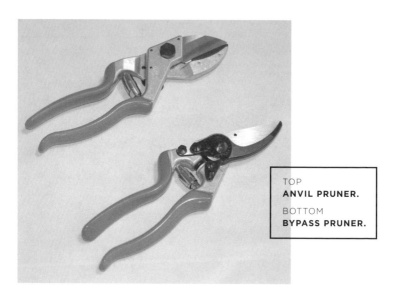

TOP
ANVIL PRUNER.

BOTTOM
BYPASS PRUNER.

A specialized type of anvil pruner is a ratcheting pruner. These pruners have a ratcheting system built into them that allows you to cut larger or harder material than you would normally be able to cut with a standard bypass or anvil pruner. This ratchet mechanism allows incremental cuts to be made by squeezing the shears and cutting a small amount with each pull. They are especially handy with hard woods and somewhat larger branches, and for people with weak hands.

REPLACEMENT BLADES AND SPRINGS. THESE ARE THE MOST COMMONLY REPLACED PARTS ON PRUNING SHEARS. MOST OTHER PARTS ARE REPLACEABLE AS WELL.

[L TO R]
ASSEMBLY GREASE KEEPS THE PIVOT WORKING SMOOTHLY AND PREVENTS WEAR; BLADE OIL KEEPS BLADES CLEAN AND SHARP FOR SMOOTHER, EASIER CUTS; CARBIDE SHARPENING TOOL; SHARPENING STONE.

Whichever type of shear you choose, it is imperative to keep the blades extremely sharp. When out in the field, it is a good idea to carry a small sharpening stone or tool to periodically dress the blades while pruning. A small can of spray on oil should also be kept on hand and the shears sprayed periodically. This not only lubricates the shears, it removes dirt that can dull the cutting edge and sap that can build up over the course of a job and create friction making cutting more difficult.

Most pruning shears can cut a branch up to 3/4 inch in diameter, larger than that it is best to move on to a lopping shear.

LOPPING SHEAR

As with hand pruners, the better the lopping shear the easier the job will be. That being said, because of their design, even a lesser grade lopper will still yield excellent results because of the cutting power they give. Loppers resemble a pruning shear with long handles allowing both hands to manipulate the tool to make the cut, bringing the power of both arms to bear on the branch. Depending on the hardness of the wood, loppers are used to handle diameters of 3/4 inch to about 1 1/2 inches. They come in a variety of handle lengths to suit the job at hand. They also come in bypass or anvil models with the same caveats as hand pruners have.

Again, keeping loppers clean and sharp will go a long way to making your pruning job much easier.

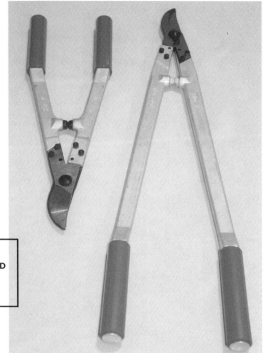

SMALL- AND MEDIUM-SIZED LOPPING SHEARS.

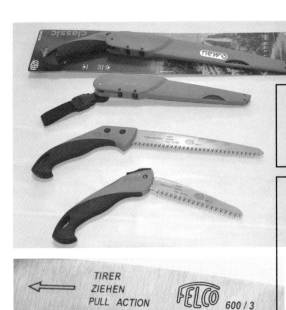

THREE SIZES OF RAZOR TOOTH SAWS.

BOTTOM FOLDING POCKET VERSION.

CLOSE UP OF THE SHARPENING TECHNIQUE OF A RAZOR TOOTH SAW. THIS STYLE OF SHARPENING MAKES FOR FASTER, SMOOTHER CUTS AND RETAINS ITS SHARPNESS FOR A LONG TIME.

PRUNING SAWS

Pruning saws are used when the size of the cut exceeds the capacity of a lopping shear. There are a couple of types of saws from smaller folding saws to larger bow saws. In pruning fruit trees and smaller shrubs, typically most cuts requiring a saw can be made using a small to medium sized saw. With the advent of razor cut teeth on saw blades, the ease of cutting increased dramatically. The razor cut style of tooth also allows for longer blade life and faster cuts. As blades wear, it is typically easier to replace the blade with a new one rather than to have a dull one sharpened. As with shears, keeping the blade clean will make cutting easier. The use of spray on oil helps immensely with this and it should be applied during and after the job to keep the blade clean and rust free. Dirt, sap and rust make cutting with the saw harder as it adds friction where the blade rubs against the sides of the cut on the branch.

Many people think that pruning roses is a difficult, technically complex job with overtones of black magic thrown in just to make it more difficult. In reality, nothing could be further from the truth. While it is true that many hardcore rosarians take great pains in pruning in hopes of growing the perfect rose for competition, the average backyard gardener can have great success with their rose garden by following a few simple guidelines. We will go over those guidelines for both new bare-root roses, established roses and light mid-season pruning on the most popular types of roses.

TYPES OF ROSES

Below are the basic types of roses that you will typically find in a landscape or garden; Hybrid Teas, Grandifloras, Floribundas, Climbing Roses, Miniature Roses, Shrub or Landscape Roses, and Ground Cover Roses. Tree Roses are typically grown with a 24 to 48 inch tall trunk grafted with a variety of bush rose to the top. The grafts are typically Hybrid Tea or Floribunda varieties and are pruned the same way bush types are.

BASIC ROSE PRUNING

Today most nurseries pre-prune and pot their bare-root roses rather than sell them truly bare-root. This was not always the case. During the bare-root seasons of yore, the roses arrived from the grower in large shipping boxes in bundles of 10. Bare-root roses are topped in the field to reduce the length of the canes but they are not pruned for re-planting. These roses were brought into the store and displayed in large bins of wet wood shavings to keep the

DORMANT ROSE
THE BEST TIME TO PRUNE ROSES IS WHEN THEY ARE DORMANT DURING THE WINTER MONTHS.

DEAD CANE
REMOVE ALL DEAD CANES FROM THE PLANT.

roots from drying out. The customer would select their rose and the nursery associate would pull it, prune it, and wrap the roots in wet shavings and heavy craft paper and send the customer off to plant it in their yard.

Now roses are still shipped as before, but instead of putting the roses into bins of sawdust upon arrival at the nursery, they are pruned and potted into 5-gallon or larger containers depending on the size of the plant. These pre-pruned roses are then ready to go home. Nurseries

CROSSING CANES
**REMOVE CANES
THAT CROSS OVER
THE CENTER OF
THE PLANT TO
OPEN IT UP.**

WEAK CANES
**REMOVE THE WEAKEST
OR DAMAGED CANES
FROM THE PLANT.**

PRUNE FOR SHAPE
**IDENTIFY THE FOUR-FIVE CANES
YOU WISH TO KEEP AND PRUNE
AWAY THE REST. YOU WANT AN
OPEN VASE-SHAPED PLANT.**

have found that by pre-pruning and planting the roses in containers in a rose potting soil, the failure rate on roses is greatly reduced and the roses get a good head start as the root systems stay more evenly moist and can begin picking up nutrients from the soil almost immediately. Roses that do not sell during the typical bare-root season of December through February already have a head start growing and can be sold as flowering specimens later in the spring.

If you purchase bare-root roses that have not been pre-pruned, the task is fairly easy. It is easier to prune bare-root roses prior to planting, as they are easily handled and you can get a good view of the plant by merely rotating it in your hand. The roses typically will have a large number of canes on them growing in various directions. Some of the canes are damaged during the digging and packing process.

Damaged or broken canes are the first to be removed and should be cut back down to their base. Once the broken and damaged canes are removed, take a good look at the plant to begin identifying the canes that will be removed and the canes that will remain. Look for canes that cross over the center of the plant or are up against other canes. These should be carefully removed, cutting them down to the base. Once the crossing canes are removed, try to identify the four to five strongest canes that remain. Picture in your mind's eye an up turned hand with fingers pointing straight up in a vase shape, or the classic caricature of a dead spider on its back with legs in the air. That is the shape you are trying to bring out. Once you identify the canes you want to keep, remove the rest following the same guidelines as before. For the canes that are left they will need to be shortened about 1/4 of their length. Examine the canes closely and you will see growth eyes or buds. You want to shorten the cane as mentioned but down to an outward facing growth eye as this is where the new growth will begin and you want It to grow away from the center of the plant to avoid crossing canes. When you make the cut above the growth eye, angle the back of the cut 30-45 degrees and about 1/4 inch above the eye taking care not to damage the eye. Not all roses are going to behave perfectly for you and have the right canes in the exact place you want them with the perfect growth eyes pointing straight out at the exact location you want to cut them. Don't fret, get them as close as you can and consider the plant a work in progress. As the roses mature they will send up more canes in different areas and continual pruning and shaping will eventually get you a very good rose bush that performs exactly how you wish.

HYBRID TEAS, GRANDIFLORAS, AND FLORIBUNDAS

Hybrid teas are arguably the most popular type of rose. To prune, the first thing you want to do is cut away any damaged, dead or broken canes. Once those canes are removed, continue by removing the crossing branches in the center of the plant and open it up. Once this has been completed, find and remove the less vigorous canes from the plant leaving four to six strong and healthy canes. Prune the remaining canes to about 10-14 inches long to an outward facing bud.

SHRUB ROSES, LANDSCAPE ROSES, AND GROUND COVER ROSES

Shrub and Landscape roses, for the most part, usually do not require the specialized pruning technique as do Hybrid Teas, Grandifloras, and Floribundas. Most of the time they really only require thinning out of dead or broken canes and pruning to shape the plants or eliminate an errant long cane. Some varieties may require cutting back the tips of the canes to remove rose hips if they are not self cleaning. Certain Shrub Roses can actually be pruned using hedge shears to shape them. Periodically you can thin out the center of the plant to remove dead or diseased canes. The same technique

SHORTEN CANES
SHORTEN THE REMAINING CANES TO APPROXIMATELY 10-12 INCHES WITH A 45 DEGREE CUT SLOPING AWAY FROM AN OUTSIDE FACING BUD.

FINISHED ROSE
AFTER PRUNING, THE REMAINING CANES SHOULD FORM AN OPEN VASE-SHAPED PLANT THAT WILL BE READY TO BLOOM IN THE SPRING.

applies to most Ground Cover Roses. Thin out dead or diseased canes, remove rose hips and keep errant or long canes controlled.

MINIATURE ROSES

MInis are pruned in basically the same manner as their larger cousins but on a smaller scale. Cut away any dead or diseased canes and eliminate canes that cross through the center of the plant, opening up the classic vase type structure. Of the canes that are left, identify five to eight of the strongest, most vigorous canes and thin out the rest.

With the canes that are left, carefully look for the outward facing bud and cut them down to that point taking care to angle the cut back away from the bud without damaging it. The canes should be shortened up about 1/3 of their length.

CLIMBING ROSES

Unlike their cousins, climbing roses are allowed to grow for two to three years prior to pruning so as to develop long canes to be trained onto trellises or walls. During this time remove only dead, diseased or unproductive canes. Once established, remove old and unproductive canes that produced no strong growth from the previous year. The remaining canes will have small side branches called laterals. Trim these laterals back, leaving two or three buds. This pruning will encourage new flowers along the canes.

TREE ROSES

Tree roses should be pruned just as Hybrid Teas, Grandifloras, and Floribundas with a bit of emphasis on keeping the head of the tree a bit spherical. This round shape is more pronounced on the tree roses as the growing part of the plant is so far above the ground. With bush type roses, you cannot get this shape due to their proximity to the soil. All dead, diseased or damaged canes should be removed and the center thinned out of crossing branches.

SUMMER PRUNING

By July, your rose garden will have gone through at least one flush of flowers, possibly more. This year's growth will have gotten somewhat long and may have crossed over the center of the plant. There will be some canes that have been cut when the flowers were taken for use in arrangements. This time of the year some of the common diseases such as Mildew, Rust and Black Spot can take hold if left unchecked. Don't be surprised if Rose Slug is evident around this time as well. By now the plants just need a little clean up to get them back on track for another round of late season flowers.

Remove any dead or broken canes and any that are growing across the center or in a direction you do not desire. Once you have done that, trim all of the remaining canes back about 1/3 their length to an outside facing bud or to a leaf with five leaflets on it; the bud will be at the base of the leaf. Part of what you are trying to accomplish this time of the year is to just clean up and fine tune the rose so you will not want or need to prune it as heavily as you do for the winter pruning. Make sure you remove rose hips and spent flowers by cutting them back to at least the first outward facing bud with five leaflets. Use your judgment to make the plant look nice when you are finished. Make sure you feed your roses once they are trimmed to encourage new growth and flowers.

About the Authors

R. SANFORD MARTIN (1900-1981)

R. Sanford Martin, author and horticulturist was born in Rochester, NY and moved to Vista, CA with his parents at the age of 10 where he developed an interest in horticulture.

While studying at University of California Farm at Davis, Martin worked at Mills Orchard Corp. Ranch in Glenn County, CA before becoming its foreman. When the Apricot production was threatened with an infestation of bacterial gummosis, Martin developed a procedure to treat the Apricots. The disease came under control with no further outbreaks occurring.

In 1922 Martin became involved in a citrus orchard in Vista and continued his study and work with citrus trees until a tractor accident halted ranch work the following year. He spent 18 years as an independent landscape architect and eventually developed a pamphlet he gave to his clients on the care and pruning of their shrubs and trees.

His first book, "How to Prune Western Shrubs" was followed by "How To Prune Fruit Trees". In addition to his interest in plant and tree care and pruning, he had a deep interest in soil and humus. He developed chemical products such as Humisite that helped prepare soil for construction, as well as Biokleen and Kilodor that addressed problems prevalent with cess pools, septic tanks and the holding tanks of recreational vehicles.

Martin was the recipient of many awards and named 'Outstanding Man of the Year" in 1975 by the Southern California Horticultural Institute.

KEN ANDERSEN OF WALTER ANDERSEN NURSERY

Ken Andersen is a third generation horticulturalist who learned his craft literally growing up in the family business, Walter Andersen Nursery. Working along side his grandfather, Walter Andersen Sr., the founder of the company, as well his father, Walter Andersen Jr., and many other family members, Ken is knowledgeable about all aspects of the nursery business. He is currently President and CEO, overseeing all nursery operations at Walter Andersen Nursery locations in San Diego and Poway, California.

Walter Andersen Nursery opened in 1928 with Walter Andersen, Sr. as its founder and owner. It started as a garden center that sold green goods, dry goods and offered landscaping services. Operation of the nursery passed to Walter Andersen, Jr. after the death of Walter, Sr. in 1983 and then to Walter's son, Ken Andersen in 2009. Many of the plantings installed by Walter Sr. can still be seen in the county, such as the Cedrus deodara along Orange Avenue in Coronado, and the landscaping at the Westgate Hotel, where the Ficus trees along the street remain.

Walter Andersen Nursery continues to be family-owned and operated with many family members employed. The nursery recently welcomed the fourth generation of Andersen's when Ken's daughter, Katy, and neice, Gigi joined the company. Walter Andersen Nursery was named one of the Top 100 Iconic Brands of San Diego by the San Diego Ad Club in 2011. Walter Andersen Nursery celebrated its 90th anniversary in 2018.

Chapters on "Backyard Orchard Culture" provided by **Tom Spellman** of Dave Wilson Nursery and Stark Brothers Nursery.

Notes